THE NEW AMERICAN FAMILY

WITHDRAWN

THE NEW AMERICAN FAMILY

JERRY FALWELL

WORD PUBLISHING

Dallas · London · Vancouver · Melbourne

144041

THE NEW AMERICAN FAMILY
THE REBIRTH OF THE AMERICAN DREAM

Unless otherwise indicated, Scripture quotations are from the New King James Version of the Bible, © 1979, 1980, 1982, 1984 by Thomas Nelson, Inc., Nashville, Tennessee. Used by permission.

Library of Congress Cataloging-in-Publication Data
Falwell, Jerry
   The new American family: the rebirth of the American dream /
Jerry Falwell.
      p. cm.
   Includes bibliographical references.
   ISBN 0-8499-3498-2
   1. Family—United States. 2. United States—Moral conditions
I. Title
HQ536.F327   1992
306.85'0973-dc20   92-34287
                                                                 CIP

Printed in the United States of America.

97 96 95 94 93 92 8 7 6 5 4 3 2 1

This book is affectionately dedicated to my
own new American Family—Macel, Jerry, Jr.,
Jeannie, Jonathan, and Jerry III.
Through the love of these, God has blessed
me with the strength to endure and
the courage to press on.

CONTENTS

FOREWORD

by
JACK KEMP

What is a family? Sometimes it seems that everyone with a political agenda has a definition to offer. Some argue that the family no longer exists, while others insist it has never changed; but all agree that the institution of the family in America is facing incredible stresses from within and unprecedented threats from without.

What has been termed the "Ozzie and Harriet" image of the family was supposed to be a group of people living under one roof: a father who worked, a mother who stayed home, and 2.5 children. That statistical model hardly fits the growing "diversity" within our culture today, but it is not entirely clear what the new standard might be. In fact, there does not seem to be a single reliable model of "family" at present.

One recent survey of the modern family comes from the Population Reference Bureau whose August 1992 report, "New Realities of the American Family," offers a perplexing portrait. Using the handful of recent *Newsweek* statistics, the report shows that 25 percent of all babies in this country are born to unmarried mothers. That represents a 250 percent increase in out-of-wedlock births in just two decades. In 1970 one child in ten was born to an unwed mother; today it is one in four. Further, the report indicates that nearly half of all children will spend a part of their growing-up years in a single-parent home.

What does all this say about our country? What are the long-term implications of these radical changes? Some of the fallout of these trends impacts the work I oversee as Secretary of Housing and Urban Development. Since 1989 I have wrestled with many of the problems facing our nation's poor urban and rural areas, including unemployment, broken families, and economic disorder. I see men and women of all classes, all races, all political and religious persuasions who are struggling to survive against the odds. I see entire neighborhoods struggling to make the American Dream a reality.

Poverty, homelessness, and crime are disabling threats in many urban centers of this nation. America's need to address the problems of our cities stands in striking contrast to the victories we have won recently in the international arena. As the world watched the march of freedom across Eastern Europe, as well as the war to liberate Kuwait, the American people sensed a new spirit of optimism and pride in their country. Once again, Americans could see themselves as the torch-bearer of freedom we have been for more than two hundred years. But we still face the problem of translating these victories into programs and policies that will help to empower our own people here in the neighborhoods and communities of America. We cannot preach freedom and democracy in Eastern Europe and the former Soviet Union unless we make it work in East Harlem, East Los Angeles, and East St. Louis. At this historic moment, when the newly-born democracies look to us for leadership, we must commit America to waging—and this time winning—a new war on poverty.

As a part of this strategy, we recognize that home-ownership has always been an essential part of the American dream; yet too many people have no homes, no apartments, no place to go. Since accepting my post in 1989, I have worked to create new jobs and policies which would encourage entrepreneurs to go into our urban areas, to help change the economic equations of despair and destitution, and to contribute to a new invigoration of business and a new level of entrepreneurship that would benefit both rich and poor. This economic component can bring renewal, but it must be available to everyone, not just the few.

The example of the Soviet Union is proof that a controlled, government-directed economy cannot work. Neither welfare programs nor tax-and-spend legislation can bring about the kinds of self-reliant and independent growth that is needed.

The American way is to make the family the beneficiary of our economic prosperity. I am convinced that business and government can only succeed when they are focused within the context of the family. If the family unit collapses, or if this touchstone of personal worth and ethical responsibility should somehow disappear, America's future will suffer irreparable damage. Our hopes for success in every sphere of life will be affected.

Even as we deal with issues such as child care, health care, job training, and all the other social issues of our day, we must also find ways of supporting and upholding the family. We must affirm its worth and its role in shaping future generations.

That is why I am happy to commend the work of Jerry Falwell in standing up for the family. Long before the foundation of the Moral Majority in 1979, Rev. Falwell was a spokesman for the American family, its hopes, its traditions, its beliefs, its needs. In ten auspicious years, from 1979 to 1989, his organization created a new awareness of conservative Christian values. It literally changed the terminology of political engagement.

Jerry Falwell created the term "religious right" to identify those Americans who cherish God and country, but who would not often be seen marching in the streets. Little by little that organization grew into a movement, and the movement swept across America. The "family values" planks of the Republican platform are a direct and obvious tribute to the work Jerry Falwell accomplished. Even though the organization that gave birth to the movement completed its mission and disbanded after ten years, its impact is very much alive and well today—and still growing.

Ironically, the "religious right" is no longer a silent majority: it has become quite vocal. Conservatives and Christians who once felt out of place in "the public square" have come forward in record numbers to express their views about the critical issues of our day. And through his work at Thomas Road Baptist Church and Liberty University, in his support of the National Association of Evangelicals, and in his frequent public speaking, Rev. Falwell continues to be a major voice for Christian principles and for strengthening the American family.

The book you are about to read is sometimes shocking, often troubling, and always compelling. Jerry Falwell offers an insightful look at the state of the family in the 1990s, a view that will challenge some and disturb others, but a view that nevertheless demands serious thought and attention. Never one for hand wringing, Rev. Falwell has issued a challenge to the people of this nation to uphold and restore the priorities of the American home and to use their voices and their votes where they count.

If this were simply a book of facts and statistics describing the crises confronting the family, it would not be the major work I believe it is. Such evidence fills the newspapers virtually every day. If it were no more than a tirade against liberal policies and government interference in our private lives, it would offer no new news. We have been struggling with those problems for years. What makes this an important book is the fact that it illustrates both the provocation and the mandate for change.

As Rev. Falwell says so clearly, "family values" means affirming the mutual bonds of commitment, love, and unselfishness ordained for the family by God. "Family values" means rearing and nurturing children in an atmosphere of love and encouragement so that each one becomes a responsible contributor to society. "Family values" also means returning to God the love and adoration He deserves for the gifts He has given so freely. After all, in the beginning God created the family.

I must also agree with Rev. Falwell that any politician or special interest lobby who protests that the term "family values" has no meaning is simply admitting that he or she does not know what it means to build a relationship in which commitment, love, and selflessness are mutual goals. Our whole concept of society begins in the family. Our ability to succeed in the world grows out of skills we learn in the home.

If Americans can mobilize behind these core values and form a coalition to uphold the American family, I believe the horizon before us is unlimited. I trust that this book will inspire and affirm many to make that choice.

═ACKNOWLEDGMENTS═

I would like to extend my sincere appreciation to Dr. Tim Clinton for his burden and vision for the family and his efforts in organizing and coordinating the research team whose efforts contributed greatly to the structure of this book. I am also indebted, again to Dr. Clinton for his skill and insight applied to the development of this book, as well as Dr. James Black and Dr. Ed Heinson. Without their expertise, it could not have been written. I also express thanks to Don Keller for his tenacity in insuring the accuracy of the references which have been quoted in these pages. And as always, I am grateful for the hard work and creativity of Randy Scott, whose business acumen has been invaluable to both Liberty University and the "Old Time Gospel Hour" for more than twenty years.

1

THE NEW REVOLUTION

T he American family is in a revolution. It is not a revolution of guns, insurrections, and rioting in the streets, but its effects can be more devastating than any coup d'état or bloody civil war. This revolution is fought with words, ideas, insinuations, and clashes over values. It is a revolution that permeates schools, legislative bodies, television shows, politics, the courts, business, and even our places of worship. It is a revolution played out in our communities, our homes, and our bedrooms. It is a revolution which will determine the fate and the future of the traditional American family.

This modern revolution weaves through every segment of American society: the media, the military, athletics, local and national government, large corporations, small businesses, the religious community, academia, law enforcement agencies, the entertainment industry, even the Supreme Court. A moral and emotional earthquake is rumbling across the land, collapsing homes, weakening values, shattering families, and threatening to crack open the very foundations of our culture.

As stark as such an image may be, let me hasten to say that this is not just the opinion of a solitary Baptist preacher crying in the wilderness. In every walk of life and in every sector of society, voices are ringing out in anger and protest. Politicians, educators, professional counselors, social researchers, religious leaders in every denomination, the people in our neighborhoods, and even writers in our secular magazines and journals are reacting with dismay to the wreckage.

Consider, for example, these words from a recent issue of *Fortune* magazine:

> The revolution in families that we see all around us—the result of an epidemic of divorce, remarriage, redivorce, illegitimacy, and new strains within intact families—has precipitated a revolution in the inner lives of our children. And a torrent of recent research makes plain that this revolution within the minds and hearts of the next generation has deeply troubling implications for the American social order.[1]

Newsweek carried a similar message:

> The numbers are daunting. There is a high correlation between disrupted homes and just about every social problem imaginable. According to research . . . more than 80 percent of the adolescents in psychiatric hospitals come from broken families. Approximately three out of four teenage suicides "occur in households where a parent has been absent." A 1988 study . . . showed that "the percentage of single parent households with [teenage] children . . . is significantly associated with rates of violent crime and burglary."
>
> A study that tracked every child born on the island of Kauai in 1955 for 30 years found that "five out of six delinquents with an adult criminal record came from families where [a parent] was absent". . . . If the intact two-parent family isn't reestablished as the dominant ideal, the effect on children will be disastrous.[2]

Recognizing the Undeniable Facts

It has become increasingly ironic, if not comical, to observe the split personality of the secular media dealing with these issues. The very writers and reporters who go to such lengths to discredit leaders, such as Dan Quayle, who stand for "traditional values," have to admit that the current course of our society is leading this nation to ruin. They say that some sort of course correction is desperately needed. In fact, they must ultimately confess that these are actually moral problems which involve fundamental issues of "right and wrong."

> *"A moral and emotional earthquake is rumbling across the land, collapsing homes, weakening values, shattering families, and threatening to crack open the very foundations of our culture."*

Even the editors of *Time* apparently agree. Commenting on the Vice President's concerns about family values, the magazine eventually admitted that Mr. Quayle did have a point when he stated, "having both a mother and a father is not some Republican affectation but an ideal to strive for. Coming into the world with one parent is a handicap, no matter how mature and moneyed the mother may be."[3]

In a recent article in *Forbes* magazine, the editors commented on these same issues in the field of education. In an article entitled "The New Conformity," Thomas Sowell writes:

The family is also under attack in our public schools. Parental authority is undermined in textbooks aimed at children as early as preschool. The theme of all sorts of so-called "decision-making," "drug-prevention," or "sex-education" programs in the public schools is that the individual child must make his or her own decisions—and must do so independently of the values taught by parents. The very concepts of right and wrong are dismissed at the outset as mere prejudices of parents or "society".[4]

Over the years, the National Education Association (NEA) and the various teachers unions have resisted every effort to include any sort of moral component in public education curricula; but even they cannot avoid these issues entirely. If administrators will not deal with them, textbook and curriculum authors must do so. The issues are so basic and so pervasive that they are core concerns of a democratic society. They simply must be addressed. In their classic text on the transitions taking place in the American family, authors Arlene and Jerome Skolnick write:

> Divorce rates first skyrocketed, then they stabilized at historically high levels. Women have surged into the work place. Birth rates have declined. The women's movement has changed the way men and women think and act towards one another, both inside the home and in the world at large. Furthermore, social and sexual rules that once seemed carved in stone have crumbled away.[5]

In addition, they add, "living together" has become socially acceptable, abortion has become legal, and remaining single and childless is more and more common. "Over the last three decades," they conclude, "family life in America has changed so dramatically that to many observers it has seemed as if an earthquake had shuddered through the American family."[6]

Effects of the Family Revolution

I want to be quick to point out that we cannot and should not blame all of society's problems on broken families. Some people would like to use that excuse, but we have come to our current state of crisis over a long period of time and as a result of many interrelated factors. Economics certainly plays a role. So do politics, trends in education, the impact of television on both children and adults, and the rise of special interest groups and social activism over the past three decades.

All together, these factors have a combined effect which—along with an ongoing barrage of social theories and old-fashioned behaviorism from segments of the media and the universities—delivers a lethal blow to our culture. This message condones what I would call pernicious self-interest, obsessive materialism, sexual promiscuity, and open hostility to any sort of ethical authority.

To be sure, people cannot be programmed like robots or computers, and no one will be destroyed on the spot by a few messages here or there from the media or liberal educators, no matter how perverse the intent of the policies they promote. Massive social changes take time, but the cumulative effect of elemental and subtle changes eventually becomes unmanageable, and these changes have been under way for decades already.

I should also acknowledge the resiliency of the human character. We can cite many notable examples of people who have survived, even thrived on, the worst kinds of adversity. The story of a Baltimore surgeon, Dr. Ben Carson, and his rise from humble circumstances to become the top-rated brain specialist in the country is a marvelous example. Marva Collins' school for ghetto children which continues to turn out brilliant, highly motivated students year after year (against all odds and predictions to the contrary) is another. And there are many others.

Depending on how you look at it, such men and women are either heroes or survivors. They rise above great difficulties—poverty, neglect, abuse, or some form of dysfunctional family background—and go on to lead fulfilling lives. Such people have a marked influence on society. They prove that the finest achievements often, and with surprising frequency, come from the most chaotic circumstances and backgrounds. In fact, this is a testament to the miraculous way God has designed the human personality. The fact that the very things that might destroy one person can help shape someone else into a hero is nothing short of a miracle.

But such examples must not hide the fact that hundreds of thousands of men, women, and children trapped in broken homes and ruined relationships will ultimately become victims who go through life carrying the wounds of their strife-ridden families. These victims carry with them a host of problems for themselves, their communities, and their own families. They are human beings, with hopes, feelings, and dreams; but their faith has been shattered by the tragedy of their lives and the disabilities brought on by the assault on the family.

Becoming Part of the Solution

Our world certainly doesn't need any more alarmists who spread a message of gloom and doom without a single word of hope. We don't need finger-pointers who withdraw in self-righteous condescension, blaming all our problems on somebody else. I will be the first to admit that, in some ways, we are all part of the problem; but we all have an even greater opportunity to become part of the solution. What we need now are more realists who can look squarely at the facts and then look for ways to bring about important, life-saving changes to the status quo.

"Hundreds of thousands of men, women, and children trapped in broken homes and ruined relationships will ultimately become victims who go through life carrying the wounds of their strife-ridden families."

The issues confronting us today are widespread, sometimes overwhelming, and always deadly serious. They impact every segment of society, and they call for responsible action. But before we can understand the kinds of action that need to be taken, it is important that we illustrate clearly the nature of the problems. To identify some of these, consider the following:

- In 1970, 11.2 percent of American children lived in single parent homes; twenty years later that percentage had risen to 20.2 percent and, with high divorce rates and increases in illegitimate births, the number of single parent families is increasing.[7]
- Despite the genuine efforts of many single parents to provide good homes for their children, a National Center for Health Statistics reported that children from single parent homes were 100 percent to 200 percent more likely to have emotional and behavioral problems than

children from two-parent families, and 50 percent more likely to have learning disabilities.

- The sobering statistics go on. Single-parent children are twice as likely to drop out of high school as two-parent children.[8] A government survey of seventeen thousand children found that kids who live apart from a biological parent are 20 to 40 percent more vulnerable to sickness and 20 to 30 percent more likely to be injured in accidents.[9]

- Every year, over one million American children watch their parents divorce, and the effects are almost always negative. "The first reaction is one of pure terror," writes psychologist Judith Wallerstein who did a fifteen-year follow-up of 130 children of divorce.[10] Kids feel afraid, abandoned, lonely, and anxious, Wallerstein found. And the effects do not fade quickly. When compared with kids from intact families, children of divorce tend to have lower grades, difficulty relating to peers, insecurities about the future, poorer self-concepts and a greater likelihood to have their own marriages break up when they become adults.

- In one study, elementary school children from divorced homes were absent more often, had lower math and reading scores, were less popular with other kids, and more likely than others to say they were unhappy, in poor health, and dissatisfied with their lives. A recent study from Britain concludes that none of these problems for divorced children comes from preexisting problems. Notes one observer, "the most reliable predictor of crime is neither poverty nor race but growing up fatherless."[11] Add the pain that comes to the divorced couple, their parents, friends, and relatives, and the adverse effects of a failed marriage are staggering.

Life Without Father

Father absence, including the disappearance of fathers from many homes, has become "alarmingly widespread" according to the *New York Times*.[12] The statistics are changing, but when divorce occurs, most children (currently about 87 percent, according to the Census Bureau) still end up with their mothers.

A University of Pennsylvania study of one thousand children from disrupted homes nationwide found that more than half of the children whose fathers did not live with them had never been in the father's home. In a typical month, 80 percent did not stay overnight at the father's house, only one in six saw the father once a week or more, and 42 percent had not seen their fathers at all during the previous year.

How does the absence of a dad affect the kids? The compelling research evidence shows that when fathers are suddenly and permanently absent, boys ages one to two experience sleep disturbances, including difficulty falling asleep and nightmares that usually begin within one to three months after the father leaves the home. As they grow up, boys without fathers tend to be more dependent, effeminate, aggressive, and inclined to show exaggerated masculine behavior in an attempt to prove their maleness. When they become adults, these young men also have greater difficulty in relating easily with women.

Girls without fathers are affected adversely as well. Psychologist George Rekers of the University of South Carolina School of Medicine told a Congressional committee that when girls from intact nuclear families are compared with their peers, the "girls who lost their father by death were more inhibited in their relationships with males in general. . . . Girls who lost their fathers by divorce were overly responsive to males, were more likely to be sexually involved with males in adolescence, married younger, were pregnant more often before marriage, and became divorced or separated from their eventual husbands more frequently."[13]

Overall, says Rekers, the vast majority of the research shows that "children without fathers have lowered academic performance, more cognitive and intellectual deficits, increased adjustment problems, and higher risks for psychosexual development problems."[14]

All of this technical language can be summarized in these few words: When fathers aren't around, the kids suffer throughout childhood and well into their adult lives.

- Violence in American homes and in the streets is increasing steadily, has reached epidemic proportions, and now disrupts millions of lives. For many children, no place is safe. Kids are victimized at school, on the streets, and in their own homes. "An astonishing number of youngsters are beaten, maimed, molested, and murdered by parents, relatives and baby sitters," according to one report. Using data filed by all fifty states, The National Committee for the Prevention of Child Abuse (NCPCA) calculated that 2.7 million kids (that is 4 percent of American children) were abused or neglected last year. That's an increase of 40 percent since 1985.[15]

For many young people, the violence gets worse when they enter adolescence. The National Center for Health Statistics reports that homicide by firearms is now the second leading cause of death (after automobile accidents) for fifteen- to nineteen-year-old whites. Among African Americans, homicide is the leading cause of death. Altogether, 2,771 children ages ten to nineteen died from homicide in 1989. That was a rise of 48 percent from 1984. Another

2,245 in that age group died from suicide, now the third leading cause of death among adolescents.[16]

You might not have seen any of this first hand, especially if you live without teenagers in some quiet isolated neighborhood, but even as you read these words, kids throughout this country are being physically, sexually, and verbally abused in their own homes. They are being beaten and gunned down in the streets. They are severely hurting one another. And when the pressures build, they are turning the violence against themselves and taking their own lives with increasing frequency.

"When fathers aren't around, the kids suffer throughout childhood and well into their adult lives."

A New Vision for the Family

Everybody agrees: The family today is different from the way it has ever been before. Compared to bygone generations, we have more single parent families, families without kids, families disrupted by violence or divorce, blended families, and families without fathers. People are marrying later these days and are having fewer children. Unlike the homes where they grew up, many modern households have both parents working. Often parents have no alternative; they need the dual incomes to survive, even though these dual career lifestyles can put everybody under stress—especially the "latch-key kids" who come home to empty houses after school.

Overall, present day families have far more stress than previous generations encountered, in part because society to-

day moves at a faster pace, and a lot of family members feel
the pressure. Everybody seems to be in a hurry, including the
kids who are hurried into acting and thinking like adults long
before they are ready. Compared to parents in countries
around the world, American moms and dads spend the least
amount of time with their kids. And that's also less than
parents in this country spent with their kids a generation ago.

Despite the changes, however, the family is not dead and
neither is it dying. After the Census Bureau released its 1991
report, the *New York Times* ran a headline proclaiming that
"Only One U.S. Family in Four Is Traditional."[17] However,
that is misleading information and a perfect example of how
statistics can be distorted.

To understand the distortion we need to know that the
Census Bureau reports on "households." These households
include people who live with their relatives, single parent
families, single people who live alone or with roommates, and
even small communities (such as priests or nuns living in a
monastic order) or people living in half-way houses. If for
statistical purposes we define "traditional" as a married couple
living together with their children, then the newspaper reported correctly that only one in four households is a "traditional family."

But more often today, Americans marry later and live together for a number of years without children. Still others see
their children grow up and leave home, but the husband and
wife live together as "empty-nesters" into the retirement years.
According to the *New York Times* interpretation, none of these
couples who live together without children can be called "traditional." That eliminates a great number of quite normal and
quite traditional couples—including, for examples, those who
may be infertile, married couples who are waiting a while be-

fore having children, and even couples like George and Barbara Bush whose kids are grown and gone.

Out of Touch with Reality

Writers and speakers who talk about the declining American family seldom mention that, despite the increase in the number of single-parent homes, 79 percent of all families (people who live together and are related by blood, marriage, or adoption) are headed by a married couple. About half of these couples have children living at home.

"Despite the changes, however, the family is not dead and neither is it dying."

The people who advocate the kinds of social agenda which will ultimately destroy the traditional family may be in touch with the trends, but they are desperately out of touch with reality. Certainly families are not what they were a generation or two ago, but neither is anything else. I agree that we no longer have what some have called "look-alike families living in look-alike neighborhoods," and I don't think many people would want that. We want to be more than mere clones. But still, as the demographics of the "average American family" continue to change, more and more families seem to be in trouble. The Norman Rockwell image of the American family no longer exists; by and large that is a sad fact, but it is a reality we must accept.

Social activists today tell us that any group of people who have "a loving commitment" to each other are to be considered a family. Genetic kinship is not an issue, they say; traditional marriage is not a requirement, they say; definitions previously established by church, state, and historical precedent have no meaning for them. Textbooks, dictionaries, history books, and medical journals would have to be scrapped or revised to reflect their new "politically correct" image of a "family."

Like something out of Aldous Huxley's classic, *Brave New World*, the reformers hope to bring about the total deconstruction of the traditional family, but their objectives are meeting with unexpected resistance. Instead of a movement away from the family, evidence points to a swing back to more stable families and back to the "family values" that have held homes, nations, and individuals together since the beginning of time.

Consider the baby boomers. This generation of seventy-six million Americans born between 1945 and 1965 is a diverse group whose values have done more to shape the course of American policy over the past thirty years than any generation before or since. These are the children born to the generation that won the War; they were the children of the fifties and sixties; they included the hippies of Haight-Ashbury and the free speech movement of the 1970s. In some ways this is the generation which has contributed more than any other to the problems of the modern family—*but* they have also had a gigantic part to play in shaping the family of the 1990s.

In contrast to their parents, this is a generation which has been more tolerant of divorce, sex outside of marriage, cohabitation, and self-indulgent materialism. This is the generation that gave birth to radical feminism, that spawned the "sexual revolution," and that grew up under the dominant influence of television. As we will see in later chapters, the easy morality and ridicule of traditional values promoted by Hollywood and the television industry has done irreparable damage to the beliefs and values of this generation and, as a

---

"The people who advocate the kinds of social agenda which will ultimately destroy the traditional family may be in touch with the trends, but they are desperately out of touch with reality."

---

consequence, to the family. Baby boomers have grown up in a pernicious environment; and according to one recent book on the subject, this is a generation that has suddenly awakened to find itself adrift in the world. The authors describe a generation,

> without God, without one's country, and without stable families, so the people turned to the only other available alternative—themselves. When they found emptiness within and looked at their treadmill lifestyles, many have plunged into depression. But there is hope. Increasing numbers are returning to the church and finding that God is still alive and remarkably relevant. Patriotism has become fashionable again, especially in light of the Gulf War. . . . Families are changing, and family values are returning. The emptiness of individualism is slowly yielding to a greater concern for community.[18]

First Aid for the Family

Obviously, it is not possible to return to the lifestyles and the simpler way of life of the forties and fifties, and it probably isn't even desirable. Rather, we need a fresh look at the family. We need to understand its strengths and weaknesses. We need to see what lies ahead and what options are available to us. And we need to identify the friends and the enemies of the American family.

With wisdom and compassion, we need to counteract the various forces that have set their sights on destroying the traditional family and undermining the core values which once gave stability and purpose to all our lives. We must take a new and unflinching look at these realities so that we may rediscover how families can live, thrive, and grow together in a complex modern world.

That is the purpose of this book. In the pages which follow I will review each of these things in some depth. I will touch on my own view of the family by reference to my growing-up years, to some of the things my family and I have learned through our own experiences and trials, and to other things I have been able to discover through my years of ministry at Thomas Road Baptist Church and in our various educational, broadcast, and outreach ministries.

Left to their own devices, the social policy-makers will continue to chisel and blast and reshape the American family into their own image. They will tear away the old design, pulling apart the proven ways of the past in order to attach new, untested, and unreliable programs which will become the "politically correct" dogmas of the future. This simply cannot be allowed to happen. Either God in His wisdom must stop them by fierce judgment, or we must act in Christian charity to halt the avalanche of devastation wrought by the past three decades before even greater calamities come upon us.

Be assured that, in the months and years ahead, one group or the other will define the American family. Either the social activists will do it, or we will do it. Let everyone who cherishes this nation's heritage of faith and purpose hereby resolve to engage the enemy, to stop the outrages, and to restore dignity and honor to the very first social organization created by God: the family.

2

PERSPECTIVES OF A FAMILY MAN

I t happened a little after noon on Mother's Day.

According to national news reports, twenty-seven-year-old Michael Murray decided to take his two kids to the Medical Center of Massachusetts in Worcester where their mother was on duty in her job as a surgical nurse. The family wanted to drop off some Mother's Day gifts—a gold necklace with the words "Number One Mom" and a single rose.

With their mission accomplished, the father and his two children made their way back to the darkened indoor garage where the car had been parked. Murray gently set the infant seat and three-month-old Mathew on the sun roof of the car, then turned his attention to buckling Mathew's twenty-month-old sister into her seat. Without thinking further, Murray slid into the driver's seat and drove off, forgetting that Mathew was still on the roof.

Moving slowly from the darkened garage into the bright sunlight, Murray drove through busy streets toward Interstate 290. Despite heavy traffic, nobody beeped or waved to warn that something was wrong.

Pulling on to the expressway that cuts through Worcester, the driver accelerated to fifty miles an hour and then he heard it—a scraping sound on the roof of his car as the tiny seat, with Mathew strapped in, began to slide. "I looked to where he should have been," the father said later. "Then in the rear view mirror I saw him sliding down the highway." That's where he landed. In the middle of the interstate, in the path of oncoming traffic.

When I read this story in the newspaper not long ago, I could not help but feel the anguish and terror that Michael Murray must have felt as he pulled his car to the edge of the highway and bolted back to the place where his son had landed. I imagined how I might have felt under similar circumstances; shocked, stunned, already beginning to berate myself for absent-mindedly leaving such a precious cargo on the roof of my car.

I know nothing about the Murray family, apart from what I read in the papers. In their late twenties, with two kids and both parents working, they probably share child-care duties and work together to provide for their young family. It might not be easy to make ends meet—it's hard for most young couples today.

It would be tough for them to build a marriage, to juggle schedules, and to look after the needs of two small children. Living in a society where families are under constant pressure, perhaps these young people, like nearly half of all couples today, will find it harder and harder to keep their marriage together, to build their careers, to pay their bills, to guide their children through the teenage years and into adulthood.

As a husband, the father of three grown children, and a grandfather, I have deep concerns for young families. Even in simpler, less troublesome times, adjusting to the demands of home life was never easy. Learning new priorities and responsibilities, learning to give more and demand less, and learning to see things from a completely new perspective demand incredible resolve and a lot of grace.

That has always been the case. But young couples today are at greater potential risk than ever, pushed in new directions, exploited by commercialism and political opportunism, schooled in arrogant self-interest, and left to fall into harm's way by powerful forces that will certainly destroy them if they cannot react in time.

Now, this book is not a biography, and I do not want to linger on the past or on personal matters at any great length. My 1987 book, *Strength for the Journey,* was written as an autobiography and covered some of these formative experiences in more depth. But my focus on the changes within the American family gives rise to many questions which I can best address by reference to my own background. As I examine the dilemmas troubling couples and their children today, I think it would be appropriate to position some of the observations which follow in the terms I understand best: the life and struggles of my own family.

Times Were Always Tough

The first thing I must say is that times were always tough for the family. The pressures on young men and women today are unprecedented in many ways, but the obligations of marriage have always been enormous and unsettling. It is not for nothing they are called the "bonds" of matrimony. Since Adam and Eve, marriage has made uncomfortable demands on the individual. You cannot remain the same after marriage. The things that fulfilled you as a young bachelor or maiden must change, and you must consciously resolve to give up certain "freedoms" for the good of the new relationship you wish to create in marriage.

In addition, there will always be unique and unforeseen problems to deal with throughout the life of the family. I know about some of these from my own growing-up years. My father was a businessman who had interests in oil and gas, nightclubs, and real estate. He even had a hand in bootlegging and politics, cockfights, and illegal gambling—along with a variety of other enterprises.

Father grew up in the home of an atheist, and as far as I know he never went to church. He resisted my mother's attempts to discuss God during the early years of their marriage and had no interest at all in religion. Tragedies had a hand in shaping his attitudes. He couldn't understand why God would let my sister die at the age of ten, two years before my twin brother Gene and I were born. After our sister's death, Dad never trusted doctors again, and he seemed closed forever to the possibilities of the Christian faith.

Six months after the death of my sister, another crisis shattered my father's life when he shot and killed his kid brother in a restaurant just outside Lynchburg, Virginia. My uncle, Garland Falwell, was a heavy drinker who had terrorized the whole community for years. Nobody was surprised when my father was acquitted of all charges and released within days of the shooting. But I believe the memory of those events, way back in 1931, haunted him until the day he died.

My mother was another story, though. One of sixteen children, she was raised on a tobacco farm where there were few of this world's goods, but lots of love and religious devotion. Every week the family would dress up in their Sunday best and ride in the family wagon to worship at the Hollywood Baptist Church in Appomattox, Virginia. Her mother and father were serious about their faith, and here in central Virginia, where the Civil War had ended, faith and roots run deep.

Prayer, Bible reading, memorizing Scripture, singing hymns, and serving in the church were all part of my mother's upbringing. She brought this to her marriage and remained a faithful churchgoer and example of godly love throughout her life. She wasn't much interested in social events and seemed perfectly satisfied to stay at home to tend her house and family. Her compassionate and patient manner brought a stability and peace into our home that contrasted visibly with my dad's blustery, ambitious, often belligerent approach to daily life.

Looking back, I have to conclude that my father and mother were good parents. Gene and I grew up as the babies of our family with all of the privileges of our affluence, but I also came to understand how a house could be divided. From those years I gained a hard-won compassion for the divisions that tear at families today.

An Old-fashioned Revival

When I was a teenager, I often listened to Charles E. Fuller on the radio. He was the pioneer gospel broadcaster of the nation whose program, "The Old-Fashioned Revival Hour," originated from Long Beach Municipal Auditorium during World War II. I was very impressed with the sincerity of this man. The warmth and vitality of his message impressed me very much. Through those radio messages, Dr. Fuller made me aware that I was a spiritual being with spiritual needs. At the time, I didn't realize that the Holy Spirit was working through Fuller's sermons to guide me in my search for a church where the gospel was preached. But I was hungry for that something more, and I was looking for it with conviction.

Eventually I found what I was seeking in the little Park Avenue Baptist Church in Lynchburg, and in its pastor, Rev. Paul F. Donnelson. I visited there one night with my childhood buddy, Jim Moon, and I was deeply touched. Pastor Donnelson preached a moving sermon on the death, burial, and resurrection of Christ. He told us how the Savior had died on behalf of all people. He showed how God had made a way for anyone who would trust Him to have a personal relationship with God through His son Jesus Christ. It was an old message, but I was hearing it with new ears.

When the minister called us to repentance and faith, Jim Moon and I joined the eleven others who walked down the aisles of that three hundred-seat auditorium, and we placed our faith and trust in Jesus Christ. Even though I had some knowledge of Christianity and had grown up with a godly mother, I had never actually made that commitment. Today I see that night as the time and place where my walk with Christ really began.

When I first walked into Park Avenue Church, God already had a plan for my life. He had set the table for Jerry Falwell, and the direction of my life was laid out before me. I heard the gospel, I met Jesus Christ, and I began to study and read with a new hunger for the Word. I began learning the biblical principles for successful living. And later, in that same church, I met the girl who was to become my wife and the mother of our three children.

After attending and graduating from Baptist Bible College in Springfield, Missouri, and after starting the Thomas Road Baptist Church—where I continue today as senior pastor—

Macel and I were married on April 12, 1958. Since the cold January night in 1952 when we first met, I have gained a whole new understanding of what it means to be a family. Going through the early years of marriage, becoming a father, watching my kids grow into fine and responsible adults, and now seeing my grandchildren do the same has given me a profound respect—actually a reverence—for the worthy institutions of marriage and family. This truly has been the training ground of my life's work.

"Without the love that comes through a sharing, caring commitment to the family, we will always remain undernourished and unfulfilled."

Faith and Family

Today I believe with every fiber of my being that faith and family are what life is all about. Without faith and a personal, one-on-one relationship with Jesus Christ, life has no meaning. Life without Christ is just one disappointment after another leading to tragedy, despair, death, and eternal damnation. And without the love that comes through a sharing, caring commitment to the family, we will always remain undernourished and unfulfilled.

It is so painful to hear about young people today who opt out of marriage because they find it "too confining." Nothing is more hollow than that kind of empty-shell existence, but

that is precisely where the values of this self-centered generation are leading.

Macel and I were engaged within a year of my conversion
and, fortunately, her father was a loyal supporter of our relationship. Her mother, however, wasn't as sure. She had heard
rumors about my misconduct and behavior as a youngster.
Most of it was true, of course, and Macel's mother wanted to
be sure that I had really changed.

Even in those days there were enough examples of Christian leaders who had been unfaithful to their wives and who
had abandoned their families. During the time when I was in
training for the ministry, Macel and I often talked about
marriage. We were in love, but we were building spiritual
principles into our lives that would guide our lives together
and keep it strong—even before we went to the altar. Just as
I had committed my life to the full-time service of the Lord,
Macel and I committed ourselves to building a successful
marriage. And if God gave us children, we decided then that
we would strive to become worthy parents.

During those months before our marriage we made some
hard and fast decisions. We determined then that divorce
would *never* be an option. Under no circumstance, ever, would
we violate our marriage vows. For better or for worse, we
agreed to be committed to each other *until death do us part.*

We also made a commitment that we would do all we
could to be successful parents. Although we both were only
twenty-four years of age at the time of our wedding, we made
some very deep commitments to our unborn children. We
determined that we would never be absentee parents. We
determined that whatever was important to the emotional
and spiritual needs of our children would be our first ministry—ahead of the church, ahead of our own interests, ahead
of everything else.

At that time Macel was a banker. She earned more than I did during the early years of our marriage, and she was the primary contributor to our income. That was vitally important in those days. Thomas Road Baptist Church started with just thirty-five members, and when all our resources were pooled, the congregation was able to pay me a salary of sixty-five dollars a week—no fringes, no perks. Every morning, I would drive Macel to the bank, and then I would go directly to the church office. Our joint salaries were barely enough to maintain us.

Four years later, our son Jerry Jr. was born—on Father's Day, 1962. Having grown up as one of four, Macel was thrilled to have a child of her own, and she made it her goal to become a model mother. She decided to quit her job at the bank in order to give full time to raising our son. From the beginning, she was Jerry's best friend and (in my opinion) the world's best teacher.

She immediately fell in love with this new job, and she valued her duties as a mother second only to her responsibilities as a wife. Macel set a great example for our firstborn, and she taught him all the principles for successful living. I was determined to do the same. Very early, we established a family altar so we could pray, worship God, and read the Bible together. Then, two years after the arrival of our first child, Jeannie was born, and Jonathan came two years later.

Learning by Doing

When our children were growing up, it was always my practice to go to each of their bedrooms for a time of listening, talking, and praying together. Gena usually fell asleep first, so I would usually start in her room. I would ask her to tell me all about her day and what had happened. I asked her what she was thinking and what Daddy could do to help. We kissed and hugged and then I prayed again. Then it was on to Jerry's bedroom and finally to Jonathan's. Whenever I was out of town, Macel would go through this little ritual with them.

Beyond commitments of this type, Macel and I also decided that there were some things that should be special and that should be protected at all costs. The first of these was our wedding anniversary, and we made a commitment to see that our work and travel schedules would never conflict with our private celebration of that event. We did the same for birthdays and other special times in the lives of our children. We wanted to always honor the family and the special relationship we shared.

Over the years we found other ways to make it clear to our kids how important they were to us. Among them was a commitment to be there when any of the children was participating in a program, playing a ball game, or taking part in any other activity. When Jeannie studied piano and violin, for example, we went to all of her recitals. I confess that there were some close calls, and more than once there were difficult conflicts; but I am proud now to recall that we never missed a single recital.

Sometimes I think there must have been forty thousand of those performances and I didn't especially enjoy them; but Jeannie never knew it until she was well into her adult years and had begun her career as a surgeon. We also attended every kindergarten, grade school, high school, and college graduation. I am especially reminded of the time when Jerry Jr. received his law degree from the University of Virginia, since it happened on a Sunday. I was supposed to be preaching to our congregation of thousands in Lynchburg that day, but the commitment we had made more than twenty years before was that family would hold a special—even a sacred—

place in our lives. Another preacher could take my place in the pulpit that day, but no one else could be Jerry's dad at the graduation in Charlottesville.

Today our children are all married, launched into their careers, and starting families of their own. In spite of their busy personal lives and family obligations, Macel and I talk to all of our children and extended family members every day. They are still our best friends. We talk with them about everything. We do not attempt to meddle in their families and in the private issues they each deal with, but we are a part of their lives, and they are part of ours.

Our Most Important Achievements

Over the years, Macel and I have experienced both tragedy and triumph, gain and loss, sorrow and joy. We have faced praise and criticism, friends and foes; and today I cannot say whether we have gained more from the good times or the bad. But they have all contributed greatly to what we have become. They have instilled in us the conviction that God has a special purpose and plan for families, and that any force which would divide them or diminish their unity is destructive and diabolical.

God has blessed the Falwell household with the friendship of many people, and He has allowed us to lead a great local church that has had an impact far beyond our own community. Through television and radio, I have been privileged to speak to millions of people all around the world.

In the wake of events surrounding the Republican Convention in Houston, Texas, and the 1992 presidential election, some have suggested that my political activities—which would include both the Moral Majority organization and "The Old

Time Gospel Hour" broadcasts—have impacted presidential races and the growing conservative presence in Congress. Perhaps that is true; I would like to think so. But in light of the battles yet ahead of us—and the escalating attacks by anti-family activists today—this is hardly a time to reflect on that possibility. Liberty University, which we founded in 1971, has become a dynamic academic center on the East Coast and the largest evangelical Christian university in the world; but it, too, has been facing great pressures on many fronts, and no one in Lynchburg is pausing to count laurels.

In spite of the opportunities, successes, and ongoing struggles, Macel and I believe that it has been our family which has been the focus and the stability of our lives. Our children and the legacy they carry forth represent our greatest achievements. We are reminded each day that the Lord has guided and strengthened us along the way, and we know that our personal achievements have come not because of our wisdom but because of the hand of God. But without a doubt, the most important accomplishment of our lives is the raising of a godly family. Looking back over the past thirty years, I assure you we would abandon everything else at the drop of the hat for our family. Nothing could be more painful than to achieve some outstanding success, to achieve fame and recognition—to gain the whole world, as it were—but to fail at home.

For us, there can be no question about how one is successful in life. Faith and family, in that order—those must be our priorities.

Families on a Dangerous Road

Looking across the landscape of the world today, I am deeply burdened by the huge number of families in distress. Families are falling apart, pulled in every conceivable direction, struggling to stay together, trying to survive. We live in troubled times, when even the idea of "family" is being attacked openly and subtly undermined by forces—I should say, by

---

"Macel and I believe that it has been our family which has been the focus and the stability of our lives. Our children and the legacy they carry forth represent our greatest achievements."

---

crafty individuals with devious political intent—intent on eviscerating the institution of the family and discrediting its vital role in bringing stability to our culture.

Compared to the early days of my own marriage, the world we live in today is like some sort of surreal vision. This is an age of pornography and hedonism unimaginable just a generation ago. Increasing economic pressures combined with skyrocketing divorce, unprecedented levels of abuse and neglect, and rampant sexual promiscuity have created a volatile climate which eats like caustic acid into the fabric of the American home.

Today millions of kids live in homes where there are no fathers, sometimes no mothers, and no one home to provide love and guidance. Thanks to gay liberation, radical feminism, uncontrolled materialism, and political liberalism—all working against the very idea of a traditional family—young people have no concept of stability or purpose. How will they ever understand the spiritual dimensions of life when the world around them is so bleak and hateful?

Explicit sexuality, blatant immorality, and random violence roll across the screens of their television sets, grabbing their attention and shaping their minds and behavior. Like little Mathew Murray, whose infant seat landed on that dangerous road, every single American family—including yours and mine—is facing peril that could change the very landscape of our times. I am not being an alarmist. I am not reacting without provocation. Every important news magazine and every responsible professional journal in this country has cited and deplored these same conditions. While their solutions and reactions may not agree with mine, the problems are only too real. If history teaches anything, it is that the destiny of mankind is intimately interwoven with the welfare of the family. When families crumble, so do nations. As the family goes, so goes the world.

The Call to Discernment

I beg each of you to please consider the discussions in the next chapters as a serious call back to the foundational values that have kept our families strong and our nation great. This is not some plan to take us back to the 1950s, but a call to reconsider those values and principles which have always defined a fulfilled and meaningful life. Despite the messages of the media and of biological Darwinism, we are more than animals. We are more than rocks or vegetables. We are creatures of the God of heaven, endowed with judgment, reason, moral and ethical discernment, and a desperate need for purpose. These are the sensibilities and emotions which are first shaped and disciplined in the home and then schooled by the culture.

We don't live in the fifties. We live on the brink of a new century, when living is far more complex than it was in the days of my parents or yours. The world has changed dramatically in just the years since our kids were growing up. But the lessons we have learned as a people can be reapplied with godly wisdom to this world—or to any other.

God gives us discernment. Do you remember the words of Jesus to the disciples when He sent them out into the unbelieving world? He said, "[D]o not worry about how or what you should speak. For it will be given to you in that hour what you should speak; for it is not you who speak, but the Spirit of your Father who speaks in you" (Matthew 10:19–20).

We need to build new American families that rest in the deep-rooted confidence that God will guide us and provide for us when we seek to live honorably. We need the sort of time-tested biblical principles and "family values" that can weather tough times and grow through both blessing and adversity. We need families that will be as up-to-date and responsive as the latest silicon microchips, but as strong and enduring as the rock of Gibraltar.

In the following pages I will explore some of the other issues of concern to the American family today. I will offer the perspective of a family man whose life and ministry has been shaped by and committed to family values. Do not think I intend to avoid the harsh realities of daily life; I know something about these issues which are all too much a part of our world. I grew up in an alcoholic family. I also know something about the pressures that kids face today; I've got grandchildren of my own, and I have daily contact with university students.

I am aware of the pain of broken families and human failings; after all, I pastor a large church of people who live in the real world. I know firsthand about the forces in our society that are preying on the family; I have come face to face with many of the most outspoken secular leaders during my years of political activism.

I am sure there will be some who will dismiss the message of this book without ever reading a page. I am accustomed to criticism from people who are motivated by their biases and who cannot be open-minded enough to consider what a Christian conservative has to say. These are often the same "free speech liberals" who are first in line to censor and condemn their opponents.

But I have hope for the family, and that is the motivation behind this work. I have hope because we serve a God of miracles and because I know that He cares deeply for you, for your children, and for the nation we are building here. If the words alone do not convince you, let me return to the point at which I started this chapter, with little Mathew Murray on that hectic freeway in Worcester, Massachusetts.

On that Mother's Day, a retired antiques dealer named James Boothby was following the Murray car when young Mathew sailed off the roof and hit the road.

"I saw something in the air," Boothby told a newspaper reporter later. "I thought it was garbage somebody had tossed out. Then I thought it was a doll. Then I saw the doll open its mouth. I couldn't believe it. It was a little baby."

"It just landed on the road," the driver said in describing the car seat. "It bounced a couple of times, but it never tipped. It just sat right down."

As he jammed on the brakes, the older man brought his car to a screeching halt, deliberately blocking the traffic behind him. Then, jumping from his car he found an uninjured baby in an undamaged car seat and scooped him up in his arms. That day a life was saved by an incredible miracle of God. There is no other way to describe it. Is there room to hope that God may not perform just such a miracle for this troubled land?

Like baby Mathew, a lot of families are going through threatening times right now and facing imminent danger. But there is hope for the family if we act quickly.

Even before we reach the new millennium just ahead, we can build stronger, better, more stable, families. We can look to the Author and Finisher of our faith for divine guidance, and we can return to a model of fidelity and trust that once lifted this nation to preeminence in all the world. This is our only real legitimate hope, for the alternative is too grim to even consider.

3

THE TIE THAT BINDS

T he doctor will be with you in a few minutes." The nurse gave the message and hurriedly left the room.

The moments that followed seemed like an eternity as Dave Johnson's family waited for a report on his surgery. The medical team had been at work for nearly three hours, and an anxious family had spent the long morning together in a small hospital waiting room.

Dave and I were old acquaintances. We had gone to school together and had known each other since we were kids. Jean, his wife, had once been a faithful church member, but Dave's lack of interest in spiritual things and persistent problems in their family had taken a toll and Jean dropped out long ago. When the cancer diagnosis came, along with the need for immediate surgery, she called me at her husband's suggestion.

"Get Jerry to come!" Dave had told the family. "He's the only preacher we know."

I hurried over to Lynchburg General Hospital and prayed with Dave and Jean before the operation began, then I waited with the family. They were all there.

Dave's brother was there, although the two had not spoken for more than three years. Daughter Crista was there. She had married early and already had four children. Her husband, Tom, had left her a year before, but even he was there with his new girlfriend.

The Johnsons' oldest son, Bob, had caused his parents grief for years. In high school he had gotten into drugs and after leaving home for college he never came back! But Bob was there, pacing around nervously and looking as distressed and as anxious as the rest of the family.

Diane, the youngest daughter, was there as well. She had moved out two years earlier and was living with a boy whom she had met at work, but the crisis in her father's life had brought her to this crowded room where she sat on the couch, wiping her eyes and fighting back tears.

Against Desperate Odds

"Until now, I never realized how much we really needed each other," Bob remarked during the long wait. I could see the love they still had for each other and how they desperately needed one another at this time of crisis. But I could also see the emptiness and confusion in their lives. They seemed overwhelmed, without God, and so far removed from one another that they hardly knew how to talk. Now they were facing the most serious threat that their family had ever known, and they had come to support one another.

"Jerry, you don't know what it means for us to have you here," Jean said. "I don't know what we will do if Dave doesn't make it."

Being with families and caring for people in pain is part of a pastor's job. I have done a lot of it over the years, but it has never become a routine or painless process for me. I also feel the emotional turmoil in situations like this. I could feel this family's pain and fear as we clustered together to await the doctor's report.

When the surgeon finally arrived, he called us together and explained that a series of malignant tumors had been removed from Dave's chest cavity. A mass of tissue had grown around his heart and lungs, and had surgery been delayed any longer it would have been fatal. Then the doctor summarized the long and difficult treatment that would follow in the weeks and months ahead. Dave would have to undergo chemotherapy, cobalt treatment, and possibly more surgery. His chances of making it were barely fifty-fifty.

After the doctor left, I stayed to talk briefly with Jean and the children and I promised to return later that night. I especially wanted to talk to Dave when he came out of recovery. I knew the whole family would be going through difficult times, and I wanted to reassure them of my love and concern. But more than anything, I wanted them to know that they needed God at this point as never before.

"Please come back, Jerry," Jean pleaded. "Dave is going to need you. We are all going to need you!"

I assured Jean I would be back, then I suggested that we pray together and ask God for His help. As I prepared to bow my head I watched the family draw together. They had all neglected one another for years, followed their own interests and pursuits, and some had "done their own thing" to the detriment of the others. All of them had left God out of their lives. Now the children, huddled together with their arms around their mother, were facing truly desperate odds.

The Family Has Changed

As I left the hospital that day, it occurred to me that the Johnsons were typical of so many American families. They had bought into a secular philosophy that says we can each make it on our own, without God. Now that they were facing a major crisis, they realized how empty their lives had been. They needed each other, and they desperately needed God.

I have been a pastor now for nearly forty years, and I have watched generations of families come and go. I have seen families that have made God the center of their lives, families who have built their relationships upon His principles. I have watched those families in times of crisis, and even in their deepest sorrows there was joy. When troubles came, they knew how to call upon God; they knew how to support one another in their times of loss and disappointment. But I have also seen families like the Johnsons who have turned their backs on God, gone their own ways, and struggled desperately—often alone—in times of deep need. Sometimes they survive, but they do so without any divine resources to give them strength and comfort.

The "do your own thing" mentality of the 1960s has given us the "live with your own mess" condition of the 1990s. We have seen an entire generation of misguided young people grow up to become a generation of misinformed and out-of-control parents. And the results have been tragic.

Now some people are waking up to what has happened. Baby boomers, social critics, theologians, politicians—nearly everyone realizes today that we must go back to the basic family values that made our country great. The Republican party platform for the 1992 elections starts with these eight words: "As the family goes, so goes the nation." Candidates in both political parties have hammered home the importance of family values. Almost everybody, it seems, is talking about the family and about "family values."

"We have seen an entire generation of misguided young people grow up to become a generation of misinformed and out-of-control parents."

According to Everett Ladd of the Roper Center for Public Opinion Research, many Americans have "considerable anxiety" about values. People are concerned about crime in the streets, chaos in their neighborhoods, and a continual decline in the quality of public education. All of this taps into a widespread uneasiness about the state of a nation's morals and family culture.[1]

The family has always existed. It was created by God Himself when He brought the first human couple together and blessed their union with children. Throughout recorded history, we find the family as the foundational institution of society. But the family has undergone radical changes within the past two or three decades.

There's No Going Back

During the 1950s, families were very different from today. In his book, *Marriage and Family Today* author Larry Melville gives a concise historical overview of how much we have changed since those times.[2] He observes that many Americans lived in look-alike families situated in look-alike neighborhoods. In those days, America was a marriage-oriented society where matrimony was celebrated in mass-circulation magazines and in songs with lyrics like "Love and marriage, love and marriage, go together like a horse and carriage."

Of course there was unfaithfulness in those days, too. There were adultery and common-law relationships in which a man and woman would live together "in sin" and sometimes raise families. But such activities were frowned on. When actress Ingrid Bergman bore a child out of wedlock, her fans around the world were shocked and reacted with disapproval.

During those days, young people married earlier than they do today, and many started having babies a year or two after the honeymoon. Families were swollen by a large crop of "baby boom" children; schools bulged with the new burst of enrollments; and life was simpler and calmer. In the evening, families gathered around the black and white TV to watch such familiar programs as "Ozzie and Harriet," "Dobie Gillis," "I Love Lucy," and William Bendix and his costars leading "The Life of Riley."

Then came the tumultuous sixties, and the idyllic image of those "Happy Days" was smashed by a generation of young rebels who tore up our college campuses, tossed out traditional values, blatantly advocated "free sex," criticized the institution of marriage, and thumbed their noses at their own families. Hundreds of articles and books appeared with titles such as "The Crisis of the Nuclear Family," "Is Marriage Necessary?" and "Is Monogamy Outdated?"

While theologians such as England's Bishop Robinson were pronouncing the death of God, psychotherapist David Cooper wrote a book that he titled *The Death of the Family*, and humanistic psychologist Albert Ellis was pushing his ideas about how we could have sex of almost any kind, without guilt. This was the decade when church-going declined, and along with it came a sudden rise in divorce, single-parent households, and premarital sex.

During the seventies countless groups suddenly emerged with an agenda to disassemble the structures of society, to redefine the family, and to turn each segment of our culture against the other. Among radical feminists it became fashionable to attack not only traditional roles, but also the family itself. Roxanne Dunbar, one of the movement's spokespersons said, the family is "what destroys people. Women take on the slave role in the family when they have children. It's a trap."

Predictably, the 1970s became known as the "Me Decade." As the decade progressed, the new evidence was that our values were, in fact, changing. New catchwords were everywhere; words like "now," "open," "fulfillment," "awareness," and most important, "self." People read about "looking out for number one," and bought books with titles like *I'm OK, You're OK, I Just Met Someone I Like—and It's Me*, and even Jess Lair's "*I Ain't Much Baby—But I'm All I've Got.*"

Many churches began to throw out anything that was not "relevant." Business seminars taught how to climb upward even if that meant pushing others down; and somebody organized an event called an "Awareness Extravaganza." A new perfume appeared named "Me!" and new magazines were launched with names such as *People, Us,* and *Self.*

Throughout the decade people were talking about "alternative lifestyles"—meaning alternatives to traditional marriage and family values. Some of those alternatives—such as the suggestion that husbands and wives draw up a custom-designed marriage contract—were intended to help couples define their roles according to their personal preferences and abilities.

Traditional assumptions about male and female roles were often cast aside. George and Nena O'Neill's book, *Open Marriage*, catapulted to the top of the best-seller list. It stayed there for forty weeks and sold 200,000 hardcover copies with the message that old-fashioned monogamous relationships breed such "deep-rooted dependencies, infantile and childish emotions, and insecurities," that they need to be updated and replaced with exciting sexual liaisons apart from marriage. (This was a message that the O'Neills tried to rescind several years later when they realized that their philosophy had helped to destroy thousands of marriages and families).

In the 1980s the family had become a matter of intense political controversy and a battleground for reformers. In the 1980 presidential campaign, candidates Jimmy Carter and Ronald Reagan both made a point of expressing their concern about the family, although with different approaches.[3]

But throughout the preceding two decades the family had changed. Many traditional family values had been tossed aside. Idealistic baby boomers were discovering the realities of trying to survive, even in a two-income family. They were learning the difficulties of dealing with children and of coping with the stresses of a rapidly changing society faced with imminent "future shock." Old-fashioned commitment was missing from many marriages, and when things got tough, one or the other partner would usually run.

Since the mid-1960s, the word "family" has been applied so broadly and used to describe so many living situations that the term has become almost meaningless. The "Me Generation," the sexual revolution, and the most vocal and radical segment of the feminist movement had done their best to tear the nation apart. Both men and women had learned to pursue their own careers, seeking ways to find "personal fulfillment"—all to the risk of anyone who should interfere, regardless of the relationship.

Myron Magnet writes in *Fortune*: "These new beliefs about what happiness was, coupled with the belief that children's happiness was a function of their parents' happiness" had set the stage for what had become "three generations of family disintegration."[4]

Heading into the "We Generation"

Now in the 1990s, we have to live with the mistakes of the past while we try to rebuild our families for the future. It has been a long and difficult road to recovery, but today there are signs of hope. Baby boomers, long critical of the church, are returning to God.

Young parents realize that "children need a place where they can learn solid values and make friends with peers who share them," as *Newsweek* reported in a cover story about the return to religion.[5] *Time* writers described the increasing tendency of people to find simpler lifestyles where they can have "more time around home and hearth." People can't manage their homes, their work, and their personal lives while they pursue careers and yield to workaholic lifestyles. The magazine concludes:

As a result, many working mothers (and some fathers) are giving up full-time careers to devote more time to home life. "There is a sense of an enormous trade-off between a fast-track career and family well-being," says economist Sylvia Ann Hewlette, author of . . . *When the Bough Breaks: The Cost of Neglecting Our Children*. "Women can see the damage all around them and are making different choices than they did a few years ago." Some couples are even thinking twice about divorce in light of the problems it can pose for children, the financial damage it does to families and the other consequences. The U.S. divorce rate, which reached a high of 5.3 per 1,000 people in 1979, is now 4.7 and may still be falling.[6]

The magazine's writers note that people today want some kind of purpose and direction for their lives. They want to know "Who am I?" and "Where am I going?" So many are returning to the idea of helping others that some social observers have already begun calling the 1990s the "We Decade."

Even more surprising, though, is the conclusion of a sociologist writing in the professional *Journal of Marriage and the Family*. The author documents the well-established fact that children from single-parent families have less success in school and, ultimately, have lower earnings and poorer jobs than children reared in intact, two-parent families. Then, in the scholar's professional jargon, he suggests that:

> One reason why children of one-parent families achieve less as adults is that they lack exposure to hierarchical models of authority relations in their families. The family serves as the prototype of all authority relationships. By virtue of living in nonhierarchical families, children from single-parent households are handicapped in their ability to function in institutions that are fundamentally hierarchical, namely, education, the economy, and occupations.[7]

Despite each of these various concerns and the related glimmers of hope, many forces still actively work in this country to destroy families. In later chapters we will look carefully at some of these enemies of the family and see how they are affecting our homes, our children, and our nation. But first we must answer two basic questions. What is a family and what purpose does the family serve?

> **"According to the Bible, God decreed just three institutions; the family, the church, and government."**

What Is the Family?

According to the Bible, God decreed just three institutions; the family, the church, and government. The family is a God-ordained institution founded upon the marriage of one man and one woman, promising to remain faithful for life as husband and wife, and committed to one another for the purposes of mutual love and the raising of their biological or adopted children, should these come into their lives. This is a definition that is biblical and a description of what usually is called a traditional "nuclear" family. Add the grandparents, aunts, uncles, cousins, and other relatives, and we have what is known as the "extended" family.

Everybody knows that a lot of families today don't fit this definition. Within recent years the family has been undergoing rapid and dramatic changes in its composition and structure. Non-traditional families are becoming more commonplace and the family of the fifties—with the husband as the sole breadwinner and the wife as full-time homemaker, wife, and mother, both living together for life and raising their children—is becoming less and less common.

Single women are having babies and adopting children. Many couples are choosing to remain childless or to delay their childbearing until they are in their thirties. The term *DINKs* has been used to identify couples with "Dual Incomes and No Kids." Such couples are not unusual now, and many choose to stay that way. All of this has led some journalists, policy makers, and others to conclude that the traditional nuclear family is like a dinosaur—a fading relic of the past.

These modern people often claim that "less than 10 percent of American families are traditional," and that the number is declining. But the 10 percent figure refers to an employed father, a stay-at-home mother, and two children who still live with their parents. If you have one, three, four or more children at home, you are not traditional, according to the widely touted definition. If you are married but without children, an empty-nest couple, or living in a single-parent home, you are considered by some politicians and family experts to be involved in a non-traditional, an "alternative lifestyle," or a "pluralistic" family. This lumps you together with gay couples, unmarried couples who live in cohabitation, and with adult students who share an apartment for a few years while they attend college.[8]

I agree with the writer who said that while the family has changed rapidly in recent years, there is good reason to "reject the myth that the traditional two-parent family has fallen so far that it is on the brink of extinction."[9] That simply is not true. Most kids today are raised in a two-parent family—even though both parents may work, one or both of the parents may have been married before, and the family size may be different from that of earlier decades.

New Family Definitions

We must agree, however, that in our culture, some so-called non-traditional families do exist, survive, and even thrive. Among this group two types of families are increasingly common. The "single-parent" family consists of one parent raising children alone, without a partner present. As we are discovering, these parents often have more difficulties than intact two-parent families, but despite their struggles (or perhaps because of their struggles), many of these families are able to provide exceptional stability for children and can meet the needs of its family members.

The same is true of "blended" families. These "Brady Bunch" families usually consist of a husband and wife, one or both of whom have been married before, and one or both of whom bring children to the new marriage. Often blended families experience difficult periods of adjustment, but success is possible. These families are involved in churches and communities. They function like traditional families, although they have come into being through remarriage.

In their recent book, *Children at Risk*, James Dobson and Gary Bauer gave a definition of traditional families that is biblical and broad enough to include natural two-parent families, single-parent families, blended families, and families with no children in the home. This definition is based on values and ideas.

Traditional families, according to Dobson and Bauer, are families where the adherents believe (1) in lifelong marriage; (2) in the value of bearing and raising children; (3) in the traditional family that consists of individuals related by marriage, birth, or adoption; (4) in the universal worth of each individual in the family, regardless of his or her productivity or other contributions; and (5) in basic values such as the importance of committing to premarital chastity, self-discipline, hard work, fidelity, and loyalty between spouses.[10]

I am convinced that traditional families like this are the most stable and most fundamental social relationship in our society, and they are far from dying out. Indeed, the future stability of our nation requires that the percentage of traditional families increase. If it should decrease, and if the biblical model of the family should fall on hard times, we will be in grave danger, with little to look forward to but moral and political collapse. And the pressures on the family are mounting in many quarters.

The Sociology of the Family

Not long ago a professor at Arizona State University wrote an article about American families past and present.[11] His conclusions are worth considering because they raise questions about whether families—strong families—are still needed today.

According to the author:

- Family life cycles have changed. Changes have occurred in the ways families develop. Compared to earlier generations, young adults marry later and have their children later (if they have children at all), grown children leave home later, older relatives live longer, and more families are divided by divorce.
- Some marriage-like behavior occurs before marriage. In 1960, less than one-half million heterosexual unmarried couples were living together; in 1988 the number had increased five-fold (to 2.6 million). Overall, marriage has become less popular among young people than it was twenty years ago.

- Fewer young children and more young adults live with their parents. In the simpler days of the 1950s, people married early and filled their homes with children. Now families have fewer children, and because marriage comes later and living at home is cheaper, more single adults live with their parents. Some are known as "boomerang" kids who left home to attend college and then moved back after the parents had become accustomed to the empty nest.
- The level of divorce has declined but is still high. Currently, about one-half of the marriages of people now in their thirties either have already collapsed or will end in divorce. But with the widespread recognition that divorce brings tremendous difficulties, many are opting to give their marriages another try.
- Nearly one-fourth of all families with children are single-parent families.
- One-seventh of the children (under eighteen) living with two parents are stepchildren. If we add people over eighteen to this number, the result is "an estimate that over one-half of today's young persons in the United States may be identified as stepsons or stepdaughters by the year 2000."
- Couples are living longer and better after their children leave home.
- Changes in family life have resulted from changes in social conditions. In the 1990s, people are better educated than they were in previous generations. More women are in the work force and they have better jobs. Difficult economic conditions and the prevalence of so many baby boomers have put stresses on family life. More families live in cities and suburbs than a generation or two ago, but families are also scattered because of

the mobility in our society. As a commentator sums up: "The average American family of today is not the same as the average family a generation ago because social conditions have changed, and family life has adapted to the new conditions."[12]

Facts like these have led some people to conclude that the traditional family is no longer needed. According to some critics, modern lifestyles, including cohabitation, have loosened family ties and shown us that people get along very well without their families. Some members of my friend Dave Johnson's family used this logic to justify their independent lifestyles—until a crisis brought them together and showed that they really needed one another.

Why Do Families Exist?

Why do we still need families? Why should they continue to exist and be strengthened? God told Adam and Eve, "Be fruitful and multiply; fill the earth." Somebody has suggested that this is the only command of God that has been obeyed happily and significantly over the ages. But many of these births are not within the confines of the family. Currently, one-third of all first births result from premarital pregnancies and more than two-thirds of nonmarital births are described by the mothers as being unplanned.[13]

Of course, many of these children are raised by caring mothers or fathers, but as hundreds of thousands of single parents know, raising a child alone is not easy—nor advantageous for the child, as later chapters will show.

When children are wanted, expected, and brought into homes offering love, nourishment, and care, the children benefit and so does the whole society. Families exist to provide the nest into which new lives can be conceived, nurtured, loved, and cared for. In other words, families are the means by which civilization and culture are preserved.

For Socialization

The family is the place where young people learn *first* and where they learn *best*. Especially in the early years when they are most impressionable, children learn about life, the world, people, trust and intimacy, responsibility, relationships, and God from the family. Here children can best learn about discipline, self-control, stress management, and how to live in a hierarchical society.

Within recent years, we have heard a lot about "mentoring" and about older people being models for those who are younger. One tragedy of the fatherless homes of today is that children in these situations have no "in-house" model of what an adult male is like. In contrast, children who grow up in two-parent families can see ongoing adult behavior, some of which they might want to forget, but much of which they later will emulate.

For Security, Support, and Encouragement

We all know that many homes are places where family members feel rejected, criticized, unwanted, and afraid. These evidences of sin and family failure do not hide the fact, however, that families are best equipped to give the security and support needed, especially in times of crisis.

The family is a shelter in the time of storm. The famous parable of the prodigal son gives a similar message. Just as the father in that story embraced his wayward son when he came home, and just as a loving God accepts and forgives us when we return to Him, so the modern family should be a place where there can be mutual encouragement and support—the kind of support the Johnsons rediscovered in that hospital room.

For Economic Cooperation

In frontier days, families who lived in little houses on the prairies worked together for survival. Today that has all changed. In many families both parents work outside the home; and as soon as they are old enough, the kids get babysitting jobs and start to work part-time in an effort to earn their own money. We don't have the same survival mentality that pulled families together in previous generations.

But families still form an economic unit. Parents are concerned about providing for their dependent children, and with increasing frequency, adult children are having to be concerned about providing for their aging parents. Financial problems can create intense stress in the home. Disagreements over money can tear families apart. Greed and the love of money can lead to all kinds of problems (1 Timothy 6:10), including problems in the home.

In contrast, economic cooperation binds couples together and strengthens family relationships. Most of us have had the experience of struggling together as families in times of real need. These hard times pull us together and help us grow.

To Give a Sense of Identity and Belonging

In a period when individuals are asking "Who am I and where do I fit?" the family can give answers. I remember my own growing-up years, discovering the various relationships in our family, and learning how the various holidays, activities, and events contributed to my sense of who I was.

When I was six years old, for example, Grandpa Falwell died and was buried in the family graveyard. For the first time in my life, I saw my father cry. Following the funeral, I remember walking past the kitchen table, loaded down with fried chicken, roast turkey, salads, hot corn on the cob, home-baked bread, and all kinds of pies and cakes and cookies. I couldn't understand why all the adults were sad and why we had all that food. I didn't grasp the sense of loss my father was feeling, but there was one thing I did understand. I was a part of that family.

"Families . . . help us define who we are, where we fit, why we exist."

The funeral, the food, and all the various related events were there to reinforce our relationship and our love and support for one another. That was the foundation upon which, later, I would learn more about my roots, my community, my religion, and my kin.

Families are like that. They help us define who we are, where we fit, why we exist. The family gives each child a name, places the child in a social class, and gives ethnic, national, and religious identity. The family plugs the child into the society in which he or she will live and grow.[14] Evelyn Duvall expresses this clearly. She writes:

Within the family, individual members can best learn the rules, rights, and obligations, and responsibilities essential for the survival of a society. . . . The kinds of praise and punishment experienced by a child in his earliest years instill in him the sense of right and wrong that he will carry into adulthood in his moral values and in his definitions of the good, the right, and the worthy. The family, functioning as a "choosing agency," evaluates and selects from among many ways of life, and so is the primary source of human values that spread outward and into society as a whole.[15]

Edith Schaeffer has spent much of her life raising her own children and speaking on the importance of the family. She has called the family a "formation center for human relationships." The family, she suggests, is worth fighting for, worth calling a career, and worth the dignity of hard work:

> [It is] the place where the deep understanding that people are significant, important, worthwhile, with a purpose in life, should be learned at an early age. The family is the place where children should learn that human beings have been made in the image of God and are therefore very special in the universe.[16]

To Give Spouses a Place for Secure, Safe Sex

Sex is a powerful drive that brings great pleasure but also has the potential for creating all kinds of personal and social problems. God knew this, so He put us into families and repeatedly instructed His people to keep sex within the bonds of marriage. Societies throughout history have concluded, too, that sex is best restricted to marriage. All known societies have put restrictions on the expression of sexuality. Even when non-marital sex has been permitted, the only form of sexuality accepted by all societies is monogamy—the sexual and marital relationship of one man and one woman.[17]

Millions of people now scoff at the idea of restricting sexual intercourse to couples within marriage, but our widespread promiscuity has led to a host of problems including the epidemic spread of AIDS. When sex is confined to marriage, the marital bond tends to be solidified and families are strengthened.

To Teach Children About God

I have spent all of my adult life pastoring a church. I believe in the church and am convinced that it changes lives and can strengthen families. Even so I agree with Charles Sell that although the church has an important place in teaching children, still "the family is the primary agent for developing a child's awareness of God." It is in the home that children experience relationships and the "spiritual sustenance that shapes their awareness of God." The home is where children learn about God, about His nature and work, and about His church.[18]

A lot of kids grow up in homes where God is ignored and spiritual issues are never mentioned. But such families are like my friends the Johnsons who came to their point of crisis without any understanding of God and who quickly turned to finding a preacher to give them help.

America was first settled by families who wanted a place where they could worship together without restriction and where they could raise their families with complete religious freedom. These families wanted to educate their children in accordance with the moral principles and values that they had come to accept as truth. Yet today, many of these same values are taught in homes, but undermined in schools, courtrooms, work places, television studios, the halls of Congress, and even on playing fields and in many churches.

The Basic Issue of Values

The cover on a recent issue of *Newsweek* magazine (June 8, 1992) was dominated by two large words printed in white on a bold red background. The words were "Whose Values?"

Inside the writer presented a thoughtful analysis of the fact that questions about values—"about how we've chosen to live our lives and how that's affected our children, about the nagging sense that unlimited personal freedom and rampaging materialism yield only greater hungers and lonelier nights—have been quiet American obsessions for some time now, the source of deep, vexing national anxiety." Commenting on a speech made by the Vice President, the magazine writer acknowledged that Dan Quayle "seems to have nudged presidential politics perilously close to something that really matters: a debate on values and the American family."[19]

The magazine raised basic questions about whose values, whose morality, whose standards of justice, whose family viewpoints we should accept. In raising these questions the author came down clearly on the side of subjectivism—that values (what is right or wrong, good or bad) depend on the individual. This is not far removed from the battle cry of the sixties when waves of college students and young adult rebels proclaimed and lived by the principle: "If it feels good, do it!"

That kind of attitude leaves us with nothing. Subjectivism gives us no firm standard against which we can test our actions and make decisions. It gives no solid basis for what we teach our children. It leaves us drifting—like much of our society has been drifting during the past several years. It reminds me of the chaotic time in biblical history when the people were without a leader, and the prophet writes, "everyone did what was right in his own eyes" (Judges 21:25).

When we cast aside time-tested values and turn them into "personal preferences" or "alternative ways of thinking," or "expressions of our personalties," we are courting chaos and leaving people adrift. Even worse, as C. S. Lewis wrote many years ago in a little book titled *The Abolition of Man*, when we abandon the transmission of values, we end with social fragmentation and risk the very obliteration of humanity.

Responding to the *Newsweek* article on values, one commentator suggested that as our fragmented society deals with the question of "Whose values?" people could begin to ask "'Who can tell me what I ought to value?' Into this vacuum step demagogues and dictators."[20]

"When we cast aside time-tested values and turn them into 'personal preferences' or 'alternative ways of thinking,' or 'expressions of our personalties,' we are courting chaos and leaving people adrift."

Already this is happening, not through generals with tanks and guns, but through television commentators and producers, professors, and classroom teachers, preachers in some of our more liberal churches, and politicians. These are people who continue to press their agendas of subjectivism, secularism, hedonism, materialism, and humanism. Some of these are people who mocked Dan Quayle when he gave a speech about values and talked about the importance of family commitments, hard work, integrity, and personal responsibility.

Quayle's speech, with its reference to fictional TV character Murphy Brown, was the brunt of numerous critical editorials and jokes from comedians. However, after the speech was reported, almost every poll showed overwhelming agreement with the Vice President. A *Houston Post* call-in poll, for example, showed 10,387 in favor and 1,866 against. That is a margin of 85 percent agreeing with Mr. Quayle.

Maybe you don't like to hear or to read political speeches and perhaps you are one of Dan Quayle's critics, but portions of his speech are worth reading, regardless of one's political preferences. Here is what he said:

> Right now, the failure of our families is hurting America deeply. When families fall, society falls. The anarchy and lack of structure in our inner cities are testament to how quickly civilization falls apart when the family foundation cracks. Children need love and discipline. They need mothers and fathers. A welfare check is not a husband. The state is not a father. It is from parents that children come to understand values and themselves as men and women, mothers and fathers.
>
> And for those concerned about children growing up in poverty, we should know this: marriage is probably the best anti-poverty program of all. Among families headed by married couples today, there is a poverty rate of 5.7 percent. But 33.4 percent of families by a single mother are in poverty today.
>
> Nature abhors a vacuum. Where there are no mature, responsible men around to teach boys how to become good men, gangs serve in their place. In fact, gangs have become a surrogate family for much of a generation of inner-city boys. I recently visited some former gang members in Albuquerque, New Mexico. In a private meeting, they told me why they had joined gangs. These teenage boys said that gangs gave them a sense of security. They made them feel wanted, and useful. They got support from their friends. And, they said, "It was like having a family." "Like family"—unfortunately, that says it all.
>
> The system perpetuates itself as these young men father children whom they have no intention of caring for, by women whose welfare checks support them. Teenage girls, mired in the same hopelessness, lack sufficient motive to say no to this trap.
>
> Answers to our problems won't be easy.
>
> We can start by dismantling a welfare system that encourages dependency and subsidizes broken families. We can attach

conditions—such as school attendance, or work—to welfare. We can limit the time a recipient gets benefits. We can stop penalizing marriage for welfare mothers. We can enforce child support payment. Ultimately, however, marriage is a moral issue that requires cultural consensus, and the use of social sanctions. Bearing babies irresponsibly is, simply, wrong. Failure to support children one has fathered is wrong. We must be unequivocal about this.

It doesn't help matters when prime time TV has Murphy Brown—a character who supposedly epitomizes today's intelligent, highly paid, professional woman—mocking the importance of a father, by bearing a child alone, and calling it just another "lifestyle choice."

I know it is not fashionable to talk about moral values, but we need to do it. Even though our cultural leaders in Hollywood, network TV, and the national newspapers routinely jeer at them, I think that most of us in this room know that some things are good, and other things are wrong. Now it's time to make the discussion public.

It's time to talk again about family, hard work, integrity and personal responsibility. We cannot be embarrassed out of our belief that two parents, married to each other, are better in most cases for children than one. That honest work is better than hand-outs—or crime. That we are our brothers' keepers. That it's worth making an effort, even when rewards aren't immediate.

So I think the time has come to renew our public commitment to our Judeo-Christian values—in our churches and synagogues, our civic organizations and our schools. We are, as our children recite each morning, "one nation under God." That's a useful framework for acknowledging a duty and an authority higher than our own pleasures and personal ambitions.[21]

Note that the last paragraph in this speech gives an answer to those Newsweek questions about whose values we should accept, whose values we should commit our lives to, and whose values should mold our families.

Family Values Are God's Territory

Truly family values, like all human values, are God's territory. These are the values that are recorded in the Bible and values that are seen most clearly in the life of Jesus Christ. His words and His life show that He valued truth, mercy, justice, individual dignity, respect for life, compassion, giving, self-sacrifice, purity, commitment to marriage and to family, religious authenticity, and both personal and national responsibility.

Jesus said, "I am the way, the truth, and the life" (John 14:6). Whoever seeks the path will find the virtue which brings peace with God, and ultimate happiness in life. I can certainly agree with the magazine writer, who says, "As 'Whose values?' becomes increasingly a cry for moral direction, Christians will want to join forces with others who want to promote honesty, sexual fidelity, family loyalty, and the dignity of work."[22]

But before we can join together to develop a new American family based on Christ's values, we need to know who is seeking to destroy family values and how these efforts are ruining lives. That will be the subject of the next few chapters.

4

MEETING THE ENEMY FACE TO FACE

N ot long ago I heard the story of a young man who is a graduate student in a major university working on his doctorate in economics. He is a brilliant student, all of his professors agree, but he carries the wounds of a broken family background deep down inside.

Stan (not his real name) was only six when his parents divorced. He was raised by his mother as an only child, but he visited his father occasionally on weekends.

In school, Stan had trouble almost from the start. He was smaller than the other kids and easy to shove around, so they picked on him. At first Stan was defensive and fought back, but in time he just gave up, withdrew into himself, and endured the verbal and sometimes physical abuse of his classmates.

Stan didn't have any friends—not even his mother, who often worked until after dark, leaving Stan to fend for himself at home. Since he didn't have a father at home, Stan had no

63

healthy male role models. Once, when his father did visit the
school, he berated Stan in front of the other students who
then had even more reason to sneer and taunt the boy.

Stan couldn't talk to his dad. When they were together,
the father preferred to watch pornographic video tapes, surrounded by a collection of magazines with sexually explicit
photographs that were usually spread throughout the apartment. It wasn't long before Stan got hooked. As a teenager
he discovered that he could make tentative friendships and
find acceptance among other guys who were obsessed with
sex and equally fascinated with pornography.

While he was growing up, Stan's mother sent him to Sunday school and occasionally accompanied him to church.
This early religious upbringing made a lasting impact on the
young man; in fact, he still goes to church in the university
community where he lives. But he continues, nevertheless, to
struggle with his addiction to pornography, and even now he
has few friends.

Stan would love to have a girlfriend. He longs for the
opportunity and ability to talk comfortably with other male
graduate students. He wants to make friends, but he remains
withdrawn. Stan, now in his twenties, is a man who still does
not really know how to relate to people. He finds it much
easier to withdraw into his books, do his research, and dream
of the day when he will be a professor who teaches economic
theory.

When Stan hears about other people's healthy families,
he quickly changes the subject. He feels such a great emptiness inside, not only because he never had a healthy family of
his own, but because he has never even seen a good marriage
or a properly functioning family. If you talk to Stan about
good families, he doesn't know what you are talking about.

Sad Realities

Unfortunately, Stan is not just a fictional character. He is a very real person struggling with the dark realities of the disintegration of the family. He longs for a family of his own, and he actually believes there may yet be one for him. But is there? Is there any hope for this troubled young man? Is there any hope for the generation of young people currently being targeted by the social reorganizers? Is there any hope for the family in America?

Today, as never before, exists a concerted effort on many fronts to destroy the traditional American family—to render it archaic and useless. Dozens of prestigious and well-financed organizations have set their sights on destroying the family. Organizations established with the express purpose of changing our traditions, beliefs, institutions, and models of behavior are already one to two decades into their plans, and advancing relentlessly.

These family enemies don't look like vampires with grotesque features. These people look like you and me, employees of government agencies, people in media, politicians and members of Congress. They are educators; even people in the church. And, by and large, they have impeccable credentials.

They are involved in influential organizations, government agencies, philosophical movements, journalistic media, and the entertainment industry. Many are family members themselves who don't even realize that their programs and political activities will eventually destroy even their own families. Others are very much aware what they are doing. Their anti-family agenda is public, clearly proclaimed in their speeches and literature, open for all to see. Who are these enemies? Let's start at the top.

Government Policy Makers

During the past two to three decades, the United States Congress has become increasingly anti-family. Despite the pro-family rhetoric of many political candidates and office holders in recent months, the overwhelming goal of liberal political issues is to wrest control of the family from fathers and mothers and put it into the hands of government.

The welfare system is a prime example. Even though government's idea of "welfare" may have started with good intentions, it quickly became an anti-family colossus that rewards women for having babies out of wedlock and penalizes unmarried mothers for marrying working husbands. Its arcane regulations and restrictions make it impossible for men and women who are doing their best to simply "get a little help." Government wants complete control, by their rules; and the regulations routinely force families deeper and deeper into the welfare trap.

In addition, the majority of the members of Congress are aggressively pro-abortion. While legislators work feverishly to block pro-family issues such as choice in education—the right for parents to choose where their children will attend school—they guarantee a woman's right to murder her children in the womb. And while they strive to promote special rights and privileges for homosexuals, they increase taxes and social restrictions on traditional families.

If government spent half as much time trying to improve conditions for the traditional American family as they spend trying to grant bona fide minority status to homosexuals, the nation would be in much better shape today. What a tragedy that lawmakers elected to serve *all the people* spend such an inordinate amount of time and tax dollars to procure rights for the relative handful of homosexuals and lesbians—and, in the process, making that 1 percent of people who have chosen a deviant lifestyle equal with legitimate minorities, such as Blacks, Hispanics, the disabled, and others.

"If government spent half as much time trying to improve conditions for the traditional American family as they spend trying to grant bona fide minority status to homosexuals, the nation would be in much better shape today."

For years now, government has attacked the family's role as the primary educator of children. The Internal Revenue Service (IRS) seeks to control private and Christian schools. The Department of Health and Human Services (DHHS) penetrates schools by redrafting textbooks, promoting "values clarification," and pushing sex education programs that purge traditional moral concepts. The entire Department of Education was created as a special favor to the National Education Association (NEA), an organization that believes that the state, and not the family, has primary responsibility for educating children.

The Changing Role of the Courts

The American system of justice was once the model for the world. Fair, logical, universal justice was a standard we demonstrated to the world, and American judges were once the epitome of sound and godly wisdom. That is no longer true.

Little by little, the courts have been eaten away by liberal values and a socialized agenda to redefine and restructure the moral systems of this nation. Court decisions have all but mandated the replacement of religion with secular humanism. Eastern mysticism, New Age pantheism, and almost any other religiously oriented philosophy is accepted freely, while anything that even hints of a Christian value system is scorned and reviled.

A recent Supreme Court decision decreed it unconstitutional for a Denver fifth-grade teacher to keep a Bible on his desk. He could not keep *The Story of Jesus* in his 240-book classroom library. A book on Greek gods, however, was allowed to stay.

I agree with the *USA Today* writer who described the Court's ruling as "a more openly hostile decision against Christianity than its school prayer ban." The same writer gave this chilling assessment of the Court's decision.

> As Bibles and pictures of Jesus sweep across the former "evil empire" of Russia, millions of U.S. school kids won't be able to hear a prayer at their graduation ceremonies. . . . At a time when blood flows in our streets and crime flourishes in corporate suites, the USA's rejection of God and religion—the foundation of a moral society—is being swallowed with hardly a hiccup from committed Christians. AIDS and condoms are in the schools, as are 135,000 guns carried in daily. Rap lyrics extolling killing, mauling women and racial hatred are heard in school hallways. Yet prayer is not welcome. If there isn't prayer in schools, there will be more prayer at funerals. Youths who can't be taught the Golden Rule will learn their own rules on our mean streets.[1]

Does this sound like something from a bad novel? Just a few years ago such a scenario would have been more appropriate in a science fiction thriller; today, it's just another story buried on page three.

Recently I came across another attempt to destroy the family. An associate at Georgetown University Law Center advocated the idea that parents should be licensed by the state. The proposal suggests that unlicensed mothers and fathers would be required to give up their children for adoption. Is this something the social engineers learned from Nazi Germany? Is it something from a handbook by Karl Marx? It certainly has the ring of a "brave new world." Such a system would destroy the rights and freedoms of parents whose ideas of child rearing are not judged to be in line with "community standards."[2]

Planned Parenthood, NOW, ACLU, and Others

Planned Parenthood is one of the most powerful and certainly the best funded anti-family organization in America today. Organized by Margaret Sanger, a radical feminist and advocate of unrestrained sexual freedom, Planned Parenthood was first granted U.S. government support on the grounds that it would help design systems to reduce illegitimacy and restore balance within the family. But these promises were merely a ruse for an insidious social agenda. As described by George Grant in his book on the organization, today the plans Sanger's group set out to accomplish have been totally reversed.[3]

Planned Parenthood received more than one hundred million dollars of your tax dollars from the federal government last year and another two hundred million dollars in private funding. The organization has alleged that public funds are not used for abortions—only the private funds are for that—but of course they keep their own books.

Planned Parenthood is directly responsible for the murder of more than eighty-five thousand unborn babies in the United States each year, and indirectly for hundreds of thousands more. There will be 1,600,000 "legal" abortions in the United States this year, as there are every year, and as there has been virtually every year since 1973. Planned Parenthood has been a ringleader of the abortion movement. When they are not directly performing abortions, suing public and private organizations over abortion, or threatening politicians and private citizens through expensive media campaigns, Planned Parenthood's operatives are busy providing both contraceptives and sexually seductive indoctrination to businesses, public and private school teachers, college teachers, poor people, and children.

Rest assured that federal taxes are not being given for these purposes, however. The government's language avoids the use of explicit terminology or references which could be emotionally or physically damaging. It is only under the disguise of such cosmetic terminology as "education" and "information" that the true agenda of the organization is carried out. Writing about Planned Parenthood's clandestine programs, one author writes:

> Everywhere this subtle and sophisticated conspiracy works to undermine marriage and family by teaching that chastity is but an "option" among many other equally valid options. Usually, pamphlets and brochures that concede that "it's ok to say no" are cited by Planned Parenthood's skilled agents when they come under fire from parents' groups or legislators for undermining traditional moral beliefs. When dealing directly with young people, they are more likely to tell them "don't let anyone cheat you out of an orgasm," and "it's alright to choose

from among numerous sex partners." Thus, twenty years after the passage of the Federal legislation for the funding of birth control clinics, every venereal disease is out of control. This was confirmed recently by the director of the Centers for Disease Control. The same people who once argued that Federally-funded birth control clinics were the best way to avoid abortion now use Federal monies to support an infra-structure which promotes abortion. Planned Parenthood alone receives the lion's share of over $140 million in Federal family planning funds each year.[4]

Underlying all Planned Parenthood programs is an essential contempt for parents. The organization asserts that parents don't teach their children about sex, that parents are likely to abuse (punish) their children for experimenting with sex, and that parents want to deny their children the pleasures of physical intimacy.

Waging War on America's Future

Every plan, every program, and every activity of these liberal organizations are designed to subvert traditional values and instill a new and godless system of values. It is nothing short of a war against America's future. And like any war, it has battle plans, destructive munitions, shock troops, and even secret operatives in every level of our culture.

We recently learned the story of a woman who graduated from college and was hired by the state of California to help solve the problem of teenage pregnancies. Soon after she started her job, a "professional" from Planned Parenthood was assigned to her. This new associate emphasized that the real problem was "to eradicate the sense of shame associated with premarital sex." The Planned Parenthood logic was obvious: "teenage pregnancy is a problem. Birth control is the solution. Shame is the barrier to applying the solution. Therefore, eliminate the barrier to applying the solution."[5]

Concerned Women for America (CWA), an organization headed by Christian activist Beverly LaHaye, now has a membership of some 600,000 members, much larger than the 250,000-member National Organization for Women (NOW)— but NOW has the ear and the support of the media. A vast majority of the national media totally agrees with the NOW agenda, and they consciously make it difficult for conservative political organizations, such as the CWA, to be heard.

At this moment I am being sued by NOW in Southern Florida because of my stand in support of the pro-life movement. NOW's attorneys are trying to use the infamous RICO laws, designed for use against "organized crime," as a legal sledgehammer against me and the others in this lawsuit. The whole case is frivolous and we will win, but it will cost a great deal of money to defend ourselves from NOW's blatant tyranny.

NOW is primarily a liberal feminist-led organization whose president, Pat Ireland, has had both a husband for many years and a female lover. "I'm not interested in hiding who I am," Ireland is quoted as saying. In the words of Gary Bauer, of the Family Research Council in Washington, D.C., "the disclosure will widen the gulf between the average American woman who rejects both lesbianism and infidelity and the feminist groups that are Washington-based and out of touch."[6]

I can only hope Bauer is right, but so far I have not seen any such movement. The NOW organization that Ireland heads is infested with people committed to adultery, lesbianism, and the perpetuation of "self" above motherhood and family. It is a militant, anti-traditional family movement. Thanks to its founders and supporters—mostly products of the hippie era—NOW has single-handedly created the war between the sexes, and I am convinced they will not stop until they carry their battle to every man, woman, and child in America.

Anti-Family Commandos

The National Abortion Rights Action League (NARAL) is another strong anti-family organization. It is the militant arm of the abortion movement, designed as a battle group to carry its pro-abortion campaign to the media, into the streets, into the schools, and into American homes. NARAL is a sister organization of NOW and a fellow traveler with more than a dozen other supporters of the liberal, anti-family movement.

The most prestigious and perhaps the most powerful of all the anti-family organizations is the American Civil Liberties Union (ACLU). From its founding in the 1930s by Roger Baldwin, the ACLU has been dominated by a Marxist/Leninist influence, and despite the proven failures of communism in the past decade, the organization continues to pursue far left socialist policies and practices.

Currently, as reported by Randall Terry in his powerful book, *Accessory to Murder: The Enemies, Allies, and Accomplices to the Death of Our Culture.* "The ACLU is the world's oldest, largest, most influential association of lawyers, political activists, and social reformers."[7] Occasionally the ACLU supports Christian cases, particularly in certain high-profile cases, but it is clear that these are largely political moves to take away their opponents' ability to show how lopsided their values truly are. They want to pretend to be impartial, to defend the exploited. But make no mistake, their platform is and has always been anti-traditional, anti-Christian, anti-family, and anti-morals.

In a recent newspaper article, Rebecca Hagelin wrote that the American Civil Liberties Union is behind the anti-God movement in this country. In the view of the ACLU, Hagelin argues, God is not "politically correct," and anyone who publicly calls upon Him must be silenced. In contrast, Hagelin writes, "Public acknowledgment of God's existence is part of our culture and our heritage. . . . Banning God from public life is the rod on which the ACLU crowd intends to hang its own version of the Iron Curtain across America."[8]

People who disagree with the opinions of these militant organizations must respond—and respond quickly—especially when we consider the strong vehicles by which these groups push their anti-family agenda: the media and the United States Government.

Anti-Family Philosophies

Most great battles are fought and either won or lost in the minds of men and women. What we think largely determines what we do and how we feel. We should not be surprised, then, to discover that much of the anti-family activism in this country is fueled by ways of thinking which are absolutely contrary to the fundamental assumptions of this nation.

From George Washington to Abraham Lincoln, the great leaders of this nation were God-fearing men who sought to incorporate in the vital documents and legislation of this nation a framework as close to the biblical view of government as possible. Today, however, leaders at every level are seeking the exact opposite. Not only are they motivated by anti-traditional, anti-family, and anti-Christian goals, but they are also dedicated to systems of thought and belief which would horrify our founding fathers.

To take the next step, it will be helpful to examine some of these ideological fallacies. And we will begin with a philosophy that is easy to recognize.

"Much of the anti-family activism in this country is fueled by ways of thinking which are absolutely contrary to the fundamental assumptions of this nation."

Self-Centered "Me-ism"

People have been selfish and self-centered since the dawn of history. All of us like immediate gratification; that is nothing new. But self-gratification as a popular philosophy gained special prominence in the 1960s and 1970s when the "Me-Generation" sprang to national attention.

These were years when baby boomers led a widespread quest for personal liberation, self-fulfillment, and self-gratification. These were years of rebellion against authority. They were years when family life seemed stifling and identified with up-tight parents with their stultifying roles and routines.[9]

Commitments to family fidelity and traditional values were tossed aside and dismissed as remnants of the past or as if part of some vague but despised military-industrial complex. At some point the battle for uninhibited personal freedom went far beyond the Constitution of the United States of America and appropriated the idea that people had rights that gave them freedom to do whatever they pleased without concern for the "common good." Ironically, those same protesters who marched under the pretense of demanding rights for others routinely violated the rights of those with whom they disagreed. They were not interested in talking about "delayed gratification"—one of the most definitive characteristics of a civilized society—instead, they chanted, "We want it all, and we want it now!"

Professor and best-selling author Allan Bloom once asked a class of university students why fathers used to reject wayward daughters but today rarely protest when boyfriends spend the night in their homes: "A very nice, very normal, young woman responded, 'Because it's no big deal.'"[10] Unfortunately, sex outside of marriage is no big deal to the Me Generation. Just look at the number of unmarried couples who "live together," in part because they claim this is their *right* and because they don't have to wait.

Television actors, movie stars, rock musicians, and all the popular idols of the day reinforce these self-destructive images and attitudes. During one recent television season, unmarried partners outnumbered married partners twenty-four to one, with nobody expressing concern about birth control or sexually transmitted disease. Every year, television characters have intercourse (rarely with married partners) twenty thousand times, but nobody gets pregnant and nobody gets AIDS.[11] This kind of message gives clear support to the idea that the only standard of right and wrong is what feels good.

"Me-ism" is also a big part of today's growing divorce rate. The emphasis is not upon divorce but upon "easy divorce" that terminates a marital commitment with minimum inconvenience. Little serious effort is devoted to working out difficulties or to trying to maintain the permanency of marriage. In a culture that emphasizes making divorce easy, comfortable, and relatively painless, self-centered "me-ism" becomes a deadly force.

Secular Humanism

Humanism began during the Renaissance as a Christian expression of appreciation for the human beings that God had created. As it progressed over the years, however, humanism gave increasing attention to the glory of humanity and less to the glory of God. What began as theism became atheism. In place of divine revelation as a guide for thought and life, authority was transferred to human reason and scientific innovation.

"Humanism leaves society
with no anchor to give stability
to its decisions.
In this value system,
nothing is sacred."

Eventually, human beings were no longer seen as beings created in the image of God. Instead we were viewed as the products of evolution. Douglas Groothuis observes: "Morality was severed from its absolute, universal reference to God; instead it was determined by the whims of humanity."[12] Commitment to moral absolutes was replaced by me-centered relativism.

The atheistic philosophy of secular humanism has had a powerful impact on society and on family. By teaching that God is dead and that each of us must find our own ethical standards, the humanist has left an entire generation afloat in a sea of moral debate tossed to and fro by currents of moral uncertainty. Humanism leaves society with no anchor to give stability to its decisions.

In this value system, nothing is sacred. Every person can choose his or her own values and all choices are equal, with one notable exception: The only ones deemed unacceptable are traditional Christian values. These open-minded secular humanists have no place in their philosophy for the Christian world view.

Consider how this cult of atheism has influenced education. In public schools, parental authority and family roles are undermined as children are taught to make their own decisions independently of the values taught by their parents. The very concepts of "right and wrong" are being discarded as mere prejudices of parents or "society."[13]

The truly important values of society are turned topsy turvy. Matters which involve conscience, character, and culture are tossed aside as "too confining" or "too judgmental." Writing in the *Washington Post*, Richard Cohen notes, "[T]he penchant to praise and to build self-esteem has produced an academic culture that values the little smile sticker on a test paper more than the knowledge itself. It's not what you know that counts, it's how you feel about it."[14]

Our educational system has slid so far down the slippery slope of secular humanism that even the students give up. Right now some 25 percent of all students will drop out of high school, and the figure is as high as 50 percent in poor and minority areas.[15]

The Humanist Agenda in the Schools

Many public school teachers and administrators are imprisoned by the gurus of progressive education. The courts have tied their hands. They cannot teach values, they dare not mention the existence of God, and actual discipline is out of the question. These public school educators would like to see a return to the day when God was at the center of educational values in this country, but that seems an impossible dream. Because of the ACLU and other anti-family, anti-children organizations—aided and abetted by the courts—it is no longer possible to point to the religious heritage of this country in America's public schools.

The debate over values in education continues even more visibly over the issue of sex education. On one side are the humanistic thinkers who maintain that sex before marriage is both acceptable and prevalent. These social theorists argue that sex education is needed to stop the surging numbers of pregnancies, venereal infections, and abortions. To these people, sex education means teaching young people about explicit sexual behaviors in an effort to save lives, stem the epidemic of AIDS, and prevent pregnancies.[16]

Many of these advocates would agree with the contents of a brochure that was distributed by the City of New York and the Centers for Disease Control. This material is graphic and indecent. I caution the reader about the language which is used here, but this is what many educators and psychologists are proposing to give all of our children. I want you to know about this because this is what American children are being exposed to. Inside was a listing of "The Teenager's Bill of Rights," with six basic declarations:

I have the right to think for myself. I have the right to decide whether to have sex and who(m) to have it with. I have the right to use protection when I have sex. I have the right to buy and use condoms. I have the right to express myself. I have the right to ask for help if I need it.[17]

This brochure proclaims that "condoms can be sexy" and urges kids to "use a latex condom for any sex where the penis enters another person's body. That means vaginal sex (penis into a woman's vagina), oral sex (penis into the mouth), and anal sex (penis into the butt)."[18] This information has been given to all thirteen year olds in New York City. Is there any question why America's teens are in trouble?

The Counter Offensive

On the opposing side of the sex education debate are those who push to get sex education out of the schools. Through a growing mountain of research and documentation, opponents hope to show that sex education has been a failure from the start. Since Planned Parenthood-type programs began in 1970, unwed pregnancies have increased 87 percent among eighteen- and nineteen-year-olds.

Much of the research demonstrates that exposure to sex education is "positively and significantly associated with the initiation of sexual activity at ages fifteen and sixteen."[19] Sexually transmitted diseases and the abortion rate have both skyrocketed, and the number of unplanned births has gone up 61 percent.

The opponents of sex education have argued, so far without much response, that sex education involves paying teachers, with tax dollars, to present ideas that ridicule and reject such basic values as love, purity, faithfulness, sexual restraint, and sincerity.[20] In contrast, new evidence showing that church attendance, sex education from parents, and even race are all more effective in influencing attitudes about sexual behavior among young people than sex education curricula.[21]

While sex education continues to be both prevalent, distasteful, and an absolute failure in the schools, researchers from the National Institute of Child Health and Human Development recently tried to gain approval for a sex survey to be given to students in public school classrooms. Their questionnaire, both graphic and insensitive, was designed to question teenagers about "sexual activities, both homosexual and heterosexual, as well as contraceptive use, pregnancy, abortion and sexually transmitted disease."

According to the research designers, this survey was intended to be administered to twenty-four thousand children in grades seven through eleven. The questions pertained to the following five sex practices: (1) sexual intercourse; (2) oral sex (your mouth was on your partner's genitals); (3) oral sex (your partner's mouth was on your genitals); (4) anal sex (your penis in your partner's rectum) and (5) anal sex (your partner's penis in your rectum).[22]

Conservative Christians and pro-family groups were outraged that hundreds of thousands of tax dollars were to be spent asking seventh-graders and other teenagers if they had experienced oral, anal, or homosexual sex acts. When Health and Human Services Secretary Louis Sullivan stopped the survey, the liberal free-sex lobby and their humanist allies all over the country launched vehement protests.

The War on Human Decency

But the humanistic philosophy goes beyond the schools and reaches even into private organizations, including those designed to reinforce character and decency and self-reliance, such as the Boy Scouts. For years Scouts have recited the pledge: "I promise to do my best to do my duty to God and my country, to help other people, and to obey the Law of the Pack." But such values only irritate and incite the social reorganizers, and predictably, the Boy Scouts have come under a vicious assault.

Recently, for example, a Superior Court judge ordered a California Cub Scout Troop to readmit two ten-year-old twin boys who refused to say "God" in the Scout pledge. The Scout Troop complied with the court order, but according to Blake Lewis, national spokesperson for the Boy Scouts of America, there will be an appeal. For our recent report on these actions in my newsletter, Lewis said, "We feel very strongly about our values, and we have no intentions of letting this go on without an appeal." The Scouts have always affirmed God and country, and to allow anyone to alter those views is to break a sacred trust. Further, Lewis commented, "Mainstream American families want these values for their young people."[23]

Dr. Jack Kervorkian, the infamous "Dr. Death," portrays another basic belief of humanist ideology—the extermination of the old, the useless, and the infirm. Kervorkian believes that he has the right to help people out of their pain if they want to die. He claims to render "a medical service," and his lawyer is clear that "he's not going to stop . . . doing the right thing." Already the suicide doctor has had an impact on our society's views regarding suicide and euthanasia. The state of California will decide in the fall of 1992 if the terminally ill have the right to seek a doctor's help to die.[24]

If "assisted suicide" becomes legal—which it very well may—what comes next? Will some bureaucrat in a government office be free to terminate the lives of the mentally retarded or the physically disabled person? Will families be encouraged to terminate the lives of the elderly because they have become a burden to society? What would happen if a parent were judged to be hopelessly addicted to alcohol or a teenager were ruled incorrigible?

Even worse, what happens when society sends out the message that the "unfit and unproductive" have no right to take up space? Already many public institutions are forcing workers to retire early, to get out of the way and make room for the young ones coming up. What will become of the men and women in nursing homes? Will they volunteer to move aside and to stop being a burden to their families? Once you open the door to "death on demand," anything is possible. With its "pick your own values" philosophy, humanism ultimately permits just about any behavior if enough people agree it is okay.

The New Age Movement

Yet in spite of its pervasive influence, some have argued that humanism is on the demise. The psalmist writes, "The heavens declare the glory of God; And the firmament shows His handiwork" (Psalm 19:1). When all of nature declares the existence of God, the anti-God values of humanism must ultimately fail. But the movement back to the divine Presence is not what it ought to be; for many of the refugees from the death of humanism are fleeing, not to the God of the Bible, but to the false gods of the New Age movement.

According to author Douglas Groothuis, those who live long enough under atheism and humanism eventually slip into the philosophy of nihilism—the belief that everything is meaningless and absurd. Secular humanism has been unable to develop a compelling world view, Groothuis argues; "the acids of its own assumptions ruthlessly corrode its credibility and appeal."[25] But if each of us is autonomous and independent, then the next logical step is that we live in a universe that has no direction, no destiny, and no purpose. In such a world, the family doesn't make any sense and neither does anything else. This is obviously a dangerous and more destructive view.

But now, at a time when values have been stripped away and people's emotional and spiritual resources are at an all-time low, in comes the New Age movement, a diversified philosophy of occult and mystical spiritualism that joyfully proclaims there is a god after all. This god is all and in all. All is good, all is god, and all is one. The leading voices of the movement declare, "We are all gods!" We are all perfect, all equal, and all a part of the universal essence of god, they say.

The only problem, according to these leaders of the New Age, is that we are not aware of our divine nature. So we need "enlightenment" that leads to "a change in conscious-ness." We need what Groothuis has described as the "aware-ness of oneness and spiritual power." In time, this way of thinking leads to the belief in a coming New Age in which we will be the supra-human species we were meant to be, as superior to present day human life as humans are to apes.[26]

As this New Age influence permeates our society with its strong emphasis on Eastern religions, the traditional values of the family as a place of love, community, and shelter goes out the window, and so does most of what millions of people have lived and died for over the centuries. Clearly, the New Age movement perpetrates and complicates the disaster of human-istic thinking, and brings even greater risks for the family.

Radical Feminism

Feminism is a red-flag word that can lead to a lot of debate, anger, and misunderstanding. I agree with some of what feminists stand for. I agree that many women are lonely and frustrated in their lives. They work hard at being homemakers and mothers, but their husbands spend little time at home and never say a word of appreciation. Too often men take almost no interest in their wives or children, and the entire family suffers.

I agree that the full load of rearing a family can be a great burden, especially to a woman who is not being supported by her spouse. I agree that, like women who stay at home, women who work away from home should be respected and accorded dignity with "equal rewards for equal work." In families and nations where the Bible is believed, Christian women should expect to be honored in a very special and honoring way. In my opinion, women deserve more than equal rights in the family. But that is not what the present feminist movement is all about.

Not everyone involved in the feminist movement is a radical, but the movement as a whole supports a strong anti-family agenda. Most of its leaders would agree with Betty Friedan, founder of NOW, who once referred to traditional family life as a "comfortable concentration camp" from which women needed liberation.

This kind of thinking has led many women to see the family as a constraint. It has encouraged others to place greater value on career achievements than on bringing up the next generation. It has belittled those women who choose to be homemakers committed to raising and nurturing their own children. In the words of Dr. Mary Jo Bane, associate director of Wellesley College's Center for Research on Women, "The fact that children are raised in families means there's no equality. . . . in order to raise children with equality, we must take them away from families and raise them . . . "[27]

Because they build much of their thinking on humanism, leaders in the feminist movement have no place for God. Gloria Steinem, former editor of *Ms* magazine is reported to have said, "By the year 2000 we will, I hope, raise our children to believe in human potential, not God . . ." Apparently Betty Friedan agrees. She was a signer of the *Humanist Manifesto II*, which contains the statement that "No deity will save us, we must save ourselves. Promises of immortal salvation or fear of eternal damnation are both illusory and harmful."[28]

More recently a writer for the *Los Angeles Times* argued that "traditional family values is a right-wing euphemism for 'a white family where Daddy's the boss.' . . . Our country's government is not pro-motherhood or even pro-parenthood. It's anti-choice, pro-married and in favor of 'traditional motherhood' because the guys in government want the old fairy-tale days back."[29] Many of us would argue that this is angry cynicism and unsubstantiated bigotry, but we could have no clearer statement of the anti-family agenda of many feminist leaders and writers.

The Sexual Revolution

Someone has suggested that three major cultural changes have been working since the 1960s to restructure and largely destroy family values in this country. We have discussed the first two of these: the Me-Generation and the radical feminism movement. Now we turn to the third: the sexual revolution that licensed promiscuity, glorified the joy of irresponsible sex and, in the words of Myron Magnet, "allowed married people to feel an unprecedented self-justification in the pursuit of sexual adventure, even if it broke up their marriages."[30]

During the past quarter century we have become a society that elevates personal stimulation and sexual gratification above mutually responsible behavior. We have bought into the major teaching of the sexual revolution that any behavior between consenting adults is acceptable.

The evidence of this vision of human sexuality is everywhere. We see it in the greater acceptance and availability of sexually explicit programming on cable television, in the movies, and on home video systems. We see erotica in the print media, in the music industry, and in advertising. In commercials hawking everything from cars and blue jeans to after-shave and beer, sex sells.

All across this nation and in every city and town you can see thousands of pornographic bookstores, theaters, and video clubs catering to so-called "mature audiences." The term "Adults Only" no longer suggests responsibility and proper behavior, but vulgar exhibitionism, erotic self-indulgence, and profanity. But age restrictions do not really prohibit the young from indulging in the same behavior. Erotic materials are easily obtained and viewed by even young children. Video rentals are not closely monitored; children quickly learn how to access the "adult channels" on their parents' TVs. In addition, what is commonly called "soft-core erotica" abounds in men's and women's magazines these days. Even comic books and PG-rated movies trade on erotic sexuality— "enough to guarantee that anyone remotely interested in viewing such materials can have the opportunity."[31]

The sexual revolution has contributed in no small way to the prevalence of cohabitation, the epidemic spread of AIDS and other sexually-transmitted diseases, the increase in divorce, the sweeping dissemination of pornography, and the gay-rights movement.

A *USA Today* article described a series of posters that appeared around San Francisco with language taken from groups that often criticize gays. One poster, labeled "The Moral Majority," pictures four young men, one of whom wears a T-shirt bearing the words "safe sex." Another poster labeled "Family Values," shows two men in an embrace. The posters are intended to promote safe sex and to congratulate men for using condoms. Les Pappas, spokesperson for a San Francisco AIDS foundation, said, "What we're talking about is self-esteem. We're saying that gay men are important, that they should take care of themselves and each other."[32]

Politicizing the Sexual Agenda

The sexual revolution has also become quite political over the past several years. Representative Pat Schroeder's Military Freedom Act of 1992 seeks to guarantee full acceptance of homosexuals in the United States Armed Forces. The bill states, "No member of the armed forces, or person seeking to become a member of the armed forces, may be discriminated against by the armed forces on the basis of sexual orientation." The bill is supported by Representatives Barney Frank and Gerald Studds of Massachusetts, both openly gay Congressman. Nationally, Schroeder's legislation has received vocal support from gay rights groups, gay veterans, NOW, the ACLU, and many other liberal organizations.[33]

Congresswoman Schroeder's activities are not limited to gays, however. When a woman was arrested by New York authorities for bringing the banned drug RU-486 into the United States to assist in aborting her six-week-old child, groups such as NOW and Planned Parenthood howled in protest.[34]

Now Representative Schroeder plans to introduce a bill that would allow women to bring such abortion pills into the country for personal use. She states, "[T]he federal government allows cancer and AIDS patients to bring small quantities of some unapproved drugs into the country for their own use, and women should be able to use the same exemption."[35]

As an interesting sidelight to this issue, the National Organization for Women recently received a 10 million dollar gift for its Feminist Majority Foundation. According to NOW sources, this is the largest single contribution ever made to a feminist cause. The gift will be used to create a center for preserving and advancing "women's rights," but one of their first projects will be applying pressure on the government to allow women to bring the banned RU-486 drug into the country for testing and distribution.[36]

Despite the negative pressure and the strong-arm tactics of its proponents, people are beginning to see that the sexual revolution has come up empty. It promises ecstasy but fails to mention the tragic results. Free sex, sex outside marriage, and exploitation of the sexual relationship for prurient or other motives leads ultimately to the debasement of both sexes, and especially women.

Jesus said, "You shall know the truth, and the truth shall make you free" (John 8:32). When enough people return to the truth of these matters, and when enough lives have been ruined by the lies of the enemy, I believe this nation will come back to its roots. I pray that it will be soon.

5

DESIRES THAT DESTROY

P erhaps nowhere can the anti-family agenda of modern secularism be seen more clearly than in the so-called sexual revolution. The degradation of morality perpetrated by this movement eats away the heart and soul of a nation and unleashes hideous monsters of death, disease, and dysfunction.

Pornography

At the center of the so-called "sexual liberation" movement is the highly profitable pornography industry which trades on exploitation and corruption. The kings of porn laugh all the way to the bank while destroying men, women, and children with equal abandon.

Perhaps Americans have not shown a strong opposition to pornography because they do not understand the full extent of what is involved. Perhaps they have not witnessed what pornography and an addiction to it can do to people. But it is high time the nation awoke and took up spiritual and political arms over this issue.

The word *pornography*, which comes from the Greek words *porne* (prostitute) and *graphein* (to write), originally referred to the activities of those who traded in sex. Twenty-five years ago the term meant writing, pictures, or other images intended to excite sexual arousal. Now the dictionary gives the word an even broader meaning: It includes arousing sexual drives that lead to "deviations, perversions and abnormal behavior."

More and more evidence today demonstrates the close link between pornography and sex crimes. For example, Michigan State Police found that pornography was used or imitated in 41 percent of all sexual assault cases investigated in that state. In North Carolina, the state police found that 75 percent of convicted sex offenders had hard-core pornography in their homes or cars.[1]

Pornography offers a dangerously distorted view of women. Sometimes they are depicted as being driven by uncontrollable lusts; at other times women are reduced to objects of masculine wish-fulfillment. Pornography destroys the privacy and intimacy of sex and, almost always, shows the sexual act as a physical relationship without love or emotional involvement.

Pornography commonly displays bizarre perversions. In some easily available periodicals, people (usually women) are shown being tortured, devoured, or mutilated. During the sex act, women are brutalized with whips, chains, and racks. Often people are pictured with abnormal sex organs. Pornography stimulates lusts which lead to actions that can become destructive habits—especially for immature and vulnerable people.

The Bible told us many years ago what would become of unrestrained lust and sexual indulgence. The Apostle James writes, "But each one is tempted when he is drawn away by his own desires and enticed. Then, when desire has conceived, it gives birth to sin; and sin, when it is full-grown, brings forth death" (James 1:14, 15). We have had nearly two thousand years to grasp this simple warning; why haven't more people listened?

"The sexual epidemic that pornography has inflicted on this nation is contributing to the rise of sexually transmitted disease, marital infidelity, divorce, and other problems even worse."

Today we are seeing the very effects described in such passages resulting from the spread of pornography. The sexual epidemic that pornography has inflicted on this nation is contributing to the rise of sexually transmitted disease, marital infidelity, divorce, and other problems even worse. Counselors increasingly encounter people addicted to pornography—people like Stan whose story I related in the previous chapter.

A variety of studies have shown that viewing pornography makes people more prone to engage in violence, including sexually-related violence, and less inclined to believe that sexual violence really hurts or is bad.[2]

But perhaps the most tragic consequence has been the impact of pornography on children. Because of the demand for pornography that portrays children, thousands of young people must be recruited to pose for pornographic pictures—

either willingly or unwillingly. There is no way of knowing just how many children are exploited and abused each day in this country, or how these young victims are affected by their involvement.

The 1986 Commission on Pornography heard reports from women who told how some of this pornographic material had affected them when they were children. Some had been brutally victimized by neighbors or relatives who drew their sadistic ideas from pornography or who used pornography to teach them "what bad girls do."[3]

In addition, many children who disappear from their homes or schoolgrounds each year may, in fact, be victims of pornographers. Some are enslaved until they are finally dumped back on the streets, useless and broken; others are simply snuffed (or killed) for the satisfaction of the sickest elements of this destructive industry.

Even as we strike out at crime, violence, social inequity, and other issues of concern, we must take action against this industry which threatens the moral fiber of our nation. Until America makes pornography unacceptable and unprofitable, we continue to place our citizens at great risk.

Abortion

Much has already been said and written about the tragedy of abortion in America, but no consideration of these issues would be complete without some further discussion. So let me touch briefly on this vital issue of our day and offer, as much as I can, a definitive perspective.

In the first place, life is a miracle that only God Almighty can create. Most responsible scientists now agree that at the moment of conception a new and unique human life is created. From that moment, any further formation of the individual is merely a matter of time, growth, and maturation. This growth process that begins at conception continues throughout our entire lives.

"Changing the language does not hide the fact that abortion terminates the life of a human being. By any definition, that is murder."

At three weeks, just twenty-one days after conception, the tiny human being already has eyes, a spinal cord, a nervous system, lungs, and intestines. The heart, which has been beating since the eighteenth day, is pumping a blood supply totally separate from the mother's. All this occurs before the mother may even be aware of the new life within her.

By the end of the seventh week that tiny creation has become a well-proportioned small-scale baby with fingers, knees, ankles, and toes. Brain waves have been recorded as early as forty-three days. By eleven weeks all organ systems are present and functioning. The eighteen-week unborn child is active and energetic, flexing muscles, punching, and kicking.

I will never be able to understand how anyone could decide to kill such a precious little child. Some who disagree with the pro-life position have criticized us for using the word *murder* to describe abortion. They argue that this is a loaded term for what they would prefer to call the medical procedure of "aborting a fetus." But changing the language does not hide the fact that abortion terminates the life of a human being. By any definition, that is murder.

In the past, America was known for honoring and protecting the right of each person to live. But today, by law, we condone more than one and a half million murders of preborn children every year, and as a consequence the entire nation is on the verge of losing respect for the sanctity of human life. We have allowed more lives to be taken through abortion since the passage of *Roe v. Wade* than through all our wars and traffic accidents combined. Surely there is something very wrong with a society that protects owls and eagles' eggs, but offers no protection for precious unborn human life. Somebody has said that the most dangerous place in America, statistically, is not on the streets or in the ghettos, but in a mother's womb. What a tragedy for America. What a shame for our world.

Recently, I read some staggering statistics regarding abortion in the United States. Most of the 1.6 million abortions performed in 1988 were on young unmarried women. Twenty-five percent of women under twenty years of age, 33 percent of women twenty to twenty-four, and 22 percent of those twenty-five to twenty-nine have 80 percent of all abortions. Further, 63 percent of all women who seek abortions have never been married, and another 17 percent are either separated or divorced. Although abortions occur all over the country (at an average cost of $298), most are performed in California, New York, Hawaii, Nevada, and Delaware.[4]

"Abortion is the only operation that can be performed on a child or teenager legally without parental permission. And approximately one-fourth of all abortions in this country are performed on women under age twenty."[5]

On a recent television special entitled "Sex Under Seventeen," several teenagers were asked why they thought so many get abortions. Their answers are revealing:

Dee: "I think that's the main way of escape."
JP: "It's almost a form of birth control."
Dee: "Birth control, exactly. 'Cause they always say you can turn to abortion."
Julie: "I've known people who have had two and just think it's nothing."[6]

When teenagers become pregnant, 42 percent choose abortion as their alternative.[7] Few of these women care about pro-life or pro-choice people fighting in the streets or battling for the support of voters and members of Congress. Instead, these women struggle with their unwanted pregnancies and often encounter pressure from their friends and parents to simply get rid of the problem.

Some pregnant women seek counseling and find counselors who are genuinely compassionate and fair, but rarely are these women informed about the health hazards of abortion.[8]

Even Planned Parenthood once warned in its literature that abortion could be "dangerous to your life and health. It may make you sterile so that when you want a child you cannot have it."[9] Even though this statement has now been dropped from their literature, the dangers still exist. In fact, abortion increases the likelihood of getting tubal infertility by 30 percent.[10]

In addition, when a woman's first pregnancy is aborted, her chances of complications in the next pregnancy doubles: miscarriage, cervical incompetence, bleeding, premature delivery, ectopic pregnancy, and post-partum complications all increase.[11] And Planned Parenthood's documents also acknowledge that abortions can also create significant trauma and depression in many women.[12]

What we must come to realize is that abortion is more than an attack on the unborn child. It is not a convenient solution to an embarrassing problem. From the very beginning, following the designs of the eugenicist Margaret Sanger, abortion was part and parcel of a much broader and more insidious plot against our traditional way of life. Robert Morrison writes that abortion is:

> a radical attack upon the political philosophy of the United States of America. To accept abortion, we must reject the view expressed in the Declaration that we are *created equal* and that our *Creator* endows us with rights that are inalienable. The abortion advocates will not stop with the choice of abortion legally secured. They have demanded and will always demand that each of us pay for these killings with our taxes. They have demanded and will always demand that hospitals—even church run hospitals—colleges and schools provide abortions. The theorists of abortion have argued quite coherently for a woman's right to sell her unborn child's organs. Further, they have argued that it is an intrusion into the constitutionally protected zone of privacy to forbid a woman to enter into a contract to conceive a child *with the express purpose of killing it and selling its organs.*[13]

This writer suggests that the twenty-first century could see a worldwide market for the "products of conception"; body parts created by the insatiable demands of increasingly decadent societies. Morrison also notes that scholars recently cited in the *Wall Street Journal* have argued that 1.5 million abortions a year may not be enough to provide sufficient fetal tissue for the burgeoning biotech industry. In time, the demand may approach three million dead babies a year.

Abortion is high on the list of anti-family enemies. Apart from the unborn lives that it ends, abortion creates untold misery that does nothing to build individuals or strengthen families. The attention it is currently receiving in the evangelical community is well deserved; our objective now must be to spread this message to the world.

Homosexuality

I have never made it a secret that I strongly oppose homosexuality. I believe it is wrong because the Bible says it is wrong, because it undermines the family, and because it violates what God has designed: one man for one woman for a lifetime.

"I believe [homosexuality] is wrong because the Bible says it is wrong, because it undermines the family, and because it violates what God has designed: one man for one woman for a lifetime."

I acknowledge that homosexuality can be complex, involving some of the deepest emotional turmoil a person can experience. For this reason we must exercise compassion toward the person, while remaining adamant in our stance against the practice. It is also important to realize that homosexual inclinations have their root in pain. These inclinations are not natural or hereditary but are the fruit of sin and tragedy—such as unfortunate or abusive early childhood experiences.

However, not all persons who struggle with homosexuality surrender their behaviors and thought patterns to their

skewcd desires. Many such people are distressed by their feelings and frustrated by feelings they have not yet been able to
change. Sometimes they decide to control their lusts, even as
responsible heterosexual people must exercise self-control. I
have compassion for them, and I believe God offers the
strength and the healing they desire. They can truly change
from within with God's help.

The homosexual activists, on the other hand, have given
in completely to their unnatural lusts and, with the support of
the liberal media, have achieved some stunning victories that
present a serious threat to the welfare of the traditional
American family.

On July 6, 1989, for example, the highest court in New
York state ruled, 4 to 2, in *Braschi v. Stahl Associates* that a
homosexual couple living together must be considered a
"family" under New York rent control regulations. And in
November 1990, the City of San Francisco adopted a "domestic partner" ordinance by referendum, permitting cohabiting couples or homosexual pairs to register their relationship
with the city for a small fee.[14] The "gay" community has a
relentless commitment to legitimizing their illicit lifestyles.

What will happen if, in fact, homosexuality should become a protected and desirable lifestyle alternative? According to one researcher, the question is not "if" but "when." In
December 1990, a major article in *American Demographics*
magazine predicted that in the twenty-first century the family
would be redefined and domestic partnerships would be recognized in all jurisdictions of the United States.[15]

No one would grant such predictions the authority of
prophecy, but evidence supports the writer's opinions. We
can see the same types of activism in the business community
that we have seen in the streets, courts, and churches of the
land. The Lotus Corporation, for example, one of America's

leading computer software developers, became one of the first major companies to establish a benefits package for "domestic partners" of company employees. Commenting on these issues, a writer in the *Georgetown Law Review* clearly spelled out the goal of these efforts. When the courts seek to preserve "traditional family" and "conventional marriage," they are denying "full humanity" for lesbians and gay men, according to the writer:

> Feminists attack the traditional family and conventional marriage as bastions of male dominance that deny full humanity to women. The traditional family and conventional marriage are hardly "sacred" institutions to those who have suffered physical violence and social and economic equality in their names.[16]

Among the essential tenets in the promotion of the homosexual movement are two often cited conclusions that (1) homosexuality is genetically caused and (2) that it involves 10 percent of the population. Neither of these conclusions can be documented. After reviewing much of the literature on homosexuality, Wheaton College psychologist Dr. Stanton L. Jones wrote that "the concept of homosexual orientation as a stable, lifelong pattern does not seem to exist in all societies, and it is rare in preindustrial societies. . . . It appears that *homosexuality can develop without genetic or hormonal factors*, but generally it does not develop without learning and socialization."[17]

The suggestion that 10 percent of the population is gay is open to formidable challenge as well. This statistic, generated by the infamous Kinsey Report, cannot be taken seriously, since it crumbles under every form of scientific scrutiny. The Kinsey Report garnered its data from criminals, including sex offenders, and then applied the results to the general population.[18]

More recent research from the University of Chicago suggests that the percentage of homosexuals in our society is much lower than the 10 percent figure. A study done by the National Opinion Research Center, which is based at Chicago, found that only 3 percent of the population claimed at least one homosexual act during 1991. Just 4.5 percent of respondents claimed some form of homosexual activity in their lifetime.[19]

Meanwhile, in San Francisco, homosexuals continue to badger the Boy Scouts over the issue of allowing gay Scout leaders to lead the troops. The Boy Scouts of America said that they will never allow homosexuals to be members or leaders. According to their spokesperson, "Homosexuality is inconsistent with the Scout oath of becoming morally straight."[20]

No consideration of homosexuality and its associated problems is complete without some discussion of the AIDS pandemic. Every news report and every survey I have read in recent months demonstrates the degree to which the AIDS epidemic is out of control. The World Health Organization (WHO) estimates that approximately ten million people may already be infected with the Human Immunodeficiency Virus (HIV).[21] It is estimated, based on current trends, that 450,000 Americans will be diagnosed with AIDS by 1993.[22]

The World Health Organization predicts that by the year 2000, at least thirty million people around the world could be affected with AIDS; other estimates suggest that, if the worst case scenario should actually happen, the number could be closer to 110 million. By the end of this decade, AIDS could become the largest epidemic of the century. It could eventually be the most devastating and most relentless killer of all time.

It is well known that AIDS began in the homosexual community, and current estimates suggest that about 58 percent of all cases can be attributed to homosexual activity.[23] But the quick spread of the HIV virus goes far beyond homosexuals. The largest percentage of growth in new cases reported today are the result of heterosexual contact among AIDS-infected carriers.

The Wages of Sexual Sin

As the prevalence of premarital and extramarital sexual activity increases, so will the statistics relating to sexually transmitted diseases (STDs) other than AIDS. Today we rarely encourage young people to "wait until marriage." Instead we encourage them to have "safe sex," using condoms. "Since sexual intercourse begins early in life," one government report concludes, "young people have a variety of partners and this leads to dramatic increases in risk of STDs."[24] Another report suggests that 63 percent of STDs occur among people who are under age twenty-five.[25]

> *"Sin always has a pricetag; and the only "safe sex" known to man is in a faithful commitment to one faithful partner in the bonds of marriage."*

The ancient disease, syphilis, which was fading away just a few years ago, has now attained its highest level of incidence since 1950, with forty-eight thousand new cases reported in 1990 alone.[26] When penicillin was introduced in 1942, the number of cases of syphilis dropped significantly;

but since 1980 there has been a 127 percent increase in all types of cases.[27]

Cases of a relatively unknown disease, chlamydia, have also exploded, with four million cases occurring annually.[28] Gonorrhea, which produces sterility in as many as 100,000 women each year, is also back on the march in the U.S., and 6 percent of women who have had just one episode of gonococcal PID (pelvic inflammatory disease) end up totally sterile.[29]

In addition, as many as ten million genital herpes infections occur each year in the United States. An estimated 16 percent of the U.S. population is infected. This involves more than twenty-five million Americans, but among some portions of the population, the infection rate is as high as 60 percent.[30]

Sexually transmitted diseases (STDs), including the fatal HIV virus, continue to be a perplexing health threat. But STDs present a needlessly tragic situation, since they are almost completely avoidable. All it takes to avoid such crippling disease is to avoid illicit sexual contact; yet, millions of people do not control their sexual appetites. Despite the risk of serious illness, sterility, disfigurement, and death, the parade of "free sex" advocates marches on, with little help or restraint from the government. Today, public health professionals even resist partner notification in known cases of HIV infection; how can we expect to show concern in any of these other cases.

In what surely is one of the saddest examples of self-centered sex, the *New York Post* reported that some men, looking for illicit sex but unwilling to take precautions against AIDS, are now turning to children. Apparently these men believe that if they can have sex with the very young children, preferably virgins, they can avoid the risk of contracting AIDS. This practice is most common in Southeast Asia; so far nobody knows just how often it occurs in America. But according to the World Health Organization, many of the children, some as young as nine, already test positive for HIV.[31] You can be certain of this: Sin always has a pricetag; and the only "safe sex" known to man is in a faithful commitment to one faithful partner in the bonds of marriage.

Does anyone still believe that condoms prevent infections? Recently in the United States, the condom has been frequently proposed as the solution to the rise of STDs and AIDS infections. But condoms cannot help if they aren't used. In study after study the evidence shows that while most sexually active people know about condoms, relatively few use them, especially among teenagers. According to surveys, fewer than half of sexually active teens use condoms, and the "failure rate" of condoms among teenagers is especially high.

Since 1970 the federal government has spent more than $2 billion to promote condom usage and safe sex. The figure topped $450 million in 1992 alone—compared to less than $8 million for abstinence-based programs that some U.S. senators have fought desperately to have eliminated. What has all of this achieved? Fifty-seven percent of sexually active teens never use condoms and many of the remaining 43 percent use them improperly or only occasionally. And what has happened to the rates of teenage pregnancy and STDs? You know the answer. Both have increased alarmingly. Dr. James Dobson has said that this is the sad "success rate" of experts who maintain that teaching about abstinence is both unrealistic and unworkable.[32]

One report concludes that men especially dislike condoms, in part because they don't want to stop to put them on. Sex is perceived by most to be instant gratification, unimpeded by precautions.[33]

Sex education teachers and other adults seem to conclude that teenagers are hardly more than animals and they are going to have intercourse regardless what they say, so they might as well promote "safe sex" by encouraging kids to use condoms. One commentator says that, "In schools the distribution of condoms has become another government-to-child operation, with parents cut out of the decisions."[34]

Even so, many have questioned what kind of a message condom-distribution gives to kids. Doesn't it convey the not-so-subtle message that "everybody is doing it," that responsible adults expect kids to have sex, and that safe sex is achievable? What often is not mentioned is that condoms give a dangerous illusion of security. The fact is condom failure rates are as high as 25 percent or more,[35] although a more realistic figure is an average failure rate of 15.7 percent, at least among married couples.[36]

It is important to note that these failures were for pregnancy prevention and not for prevention of the HIV virus. The unstated assumption in "safer sex" publicity is that the condom will be at least as effective an obstacle to HIV as it is to pregnancy. But this is simply not true. The HIV virus is a sub-microscopic .1 micron, three times smaller than the herpes virus, sixty times smaller than the spirochete which causes syphilis and 450 times smaller than sperm."[37]

Recently I read a report from a conference of eight hundred professional sexologists who were asked how many would trust a condom to protect them during intercourse with a known HIV-infected partner. Only one person raised his hand.

Economic Pressures

How does all of this influence families? Pornography, widespread abortion, homosexuality, and rampant heterosexual intercourse apart from marriage do nothing to pull families together. Instead, they lead to addictions, disease, psychological turmoil, family conflict, and sometimes deaths. The evidence is overwhelming, but the problems continue unabated.

"Baby boomers and the generation that follows will be the first in our history to have a standard of living that is lower than that of their parents and grandparents."

Sexual issues are not the only hindrances to family stability, however. For some the greatest stresses come from economics. Many modern families are fighting desperately to make ends meet and to stay alive financially. Problems are at all socioeconomic levels and in every age group, but it is the poor who suffer most, and especially the young families.

In an article titled "Whatever Happened to the American Dream?" *Business Week* magazine documents the struggles that young American families have, trying to get along financially. Citing an analysis of Census Bureau statistics, the magazine notes that if we measure using "inflation-adjusted dollars, the medium income of families headed by someone under thirty is now 13 percent lower than such families earned in 1973."[38]

This is very sobering news when we realize that, unlike the early 1970s, most young families today have dual incomes and still struggle, in part because expenses are so much higher. Over the past twenty-five years certain family expenses—housing, health care, transportation and higher education, for example—

have steadily risen above the general inflation rate. This helps to explain why in so many families both husband and wife feel they have to work to make ends meet.[39]

Washington observer Heidi Hartmann, director of the Institute for Women's Policy Research, observed that "young families are working harder for less pay," and the poverty rate for children and for young adults has increased significantly. One of the supreme ironies of recent economic developments is that while America has experienced steady growth in its Gross National Product, the economic pressures on families with children have risen significantly.[40] Things may be a little better for college graduates, but they are a lot worse for workers who dropped out of high school.

How do these financial struggles affect families? Economists widely acknowledge that baby boomers and the generation that follows will be the first in our history to have a standard of living that is lower than that of their parents and grandparents. With financial anxieties and uncertainties of such magnitude, a lot of young families will no doubt end up as depressed as their incomes. And people with less money tend to have more health problems and fewer options for getting medical help. If there are psychological difficulties and medical problems, such families encounter even more stress. Predictably, such stresses prevent the breadwinner(s) from working, and as finances get tighter a destructive cycle begins.

The Welfare Dilemma

Does welfare help? That is a complex question, but first let me say that I am not anti-welfare. Those who need help are those who cannot care for themselves, primarily the sick and the aged. As a Christian, I believe such people should be taken care of, and God will bless our country for doing so. There have been times in our nation's history when there were not enough jobs to go around, or when the existing jobs did not provide enough money to buy the food needed to keep the family alive. In such times, people have to help each other. In such times, we must help those who are able to work but, because of extenuating circumstances, simply cannot.

"The old-fashioned work ethic is a biblical principle, but today millions of citizens have found that the welfare system makes it more profitable for them not to work."

But there are deep and perplexing problems with the current welfare system. Five million people live in permanently subsidized unemployment, while our welfare rolls continue to swell.[41] In a country that has the highest crime rate in the free world, another million, mostly able-bodied, citizens loll about in overcrowded prisons where they are unable to contribute any economic support to their families or to the budgets required to support them.[42]

As a nation and as individuals, we cannot survive economically when the working population of America is faced with an ever-increasing burden of governmental spending to support a tremendously large non-working segment of our society.

The old-fashioned work ethic is a biblical principle, but today millions of citizens have found that the welfare system makes it more profitable for them not to work. And among those who do work, surveys reveal that fewer and fewer Americans want to work hard or take pride in what they do.

The very spirit that once made this country great is in danger of disappearing. Our economic engine is running down; some fear we are losing the work ethic.

Too many people who could work do not. Have they forgotten what the word "work" means? Will they live forever off give-away programs, supported by other people who work hard for a living? I have to remind people from time to time that the government does not give away anything that it does not take away from somebody else. That "somebody else" is the taxpayer.

Rising Taxes Penalize the Family

Families are overburdened because of our system of taxation. The government takes one-third of every dollar earned in the United States. According to the Tax Foundation, the typical taxpayer works from January 1 to May 12 to raise the money to pay Uncle Sam. As a result, we have less money to spend on other necessities and debts, and, in turn, families are put under even greater pressure. Our current system of punitive, increasingly confiscatory taxation, is an overwhelming burden on the family.

Citizens should share in the responsibility of paying for the functions of government, but I can testify that today citizens feel frustrated and angry at the government's misuse of their tax dollars. No power has been more abused by Congress.

Some of our money goes to support programs and activities which are diametrically opposed to the wishes of the American people. Some goes to feed a welfare system that needs to be radically overhauled or thrown out. And an increasing amount goes to pay the interest on past debts that have come about through the irresponsible spending of government.

In order to pay for its budget items—as well as a growing list of off-the-budget programs—government has been printing more and more money every year for its own consumption. Several years ago Robert Ringer made this statement:

> When a person finds that his higher income of today buys less than did his income of five years ago, he is living in a country that is being deluded and destroyed by false prosperity. He is living in a nation where the combined income of the population exceeds the total population of goods and services. He is living in a nation that is courting economic collapse.[43]

None of this is very encouraging for families, especially for younger families who face a future when financial burdens will be even greater. As we move into the next century, the numbers of senior citizens will continue to increase and a relatively small work force will be burdened with the challenge of caring for the needs of a much larger generation of older people. In addition, many of these older citizens will have expensive medical needs, and few will be paying taxes. Families that face big economic pressures today may well be facing insurmountable financial obstacles in the very near future.

Destructive Messages from the Media

Neil Postman is a professor of communication arts and sciences at New York University. His insightful book, *Amusing Ourselves to Death*, gives an interesting critique of the impact of television on our culture. Every part of our culture, he says, is touched by television. The molders of the media present an electronic stream of values, political snippets, predigested news, business ideas, and a snapshot of religion, all wrapped in a kind of showmanship that is designed to entertain rather than to inform.

The author quotes the executive editor of the *MacNeil-Lehrer News Hour* that the idea is "to keep everything brief, not to strain the attention of anyone but instead to provide constant stimulation through variety, novelty, action, and movement. You are required . . . to pay attention to no concept, no character, and no problem for more than a few seconds of time."[44]

Ninety million Americans watch television every night, and its one-way message has a profound influence on the national character. While an earlier generation dreamed of the positive values that could be instilled by this mass communications device, television has, in fact, shriveled the soul of the nation.

The television industry, controlled primarily by individuals with anti-Christian and anti-family values, has exercised commanding control over the minds of millions. People who pride themselves on free speech and freedom of thought and action, will sit compliantly in front of the tube where their values are systematically undermined, their sensitivities are dulled, and their minds are lulled into passivity.

Let us look at some examples.

- "The typical fourteen-year-old watches three hours of television daily but does just one hour of homework."[45] Before leaving elementary school, the average child in this country sees 100,000 acts of violence and eight thousand murders. On prime time, the rate of violence is five to six incidents every hour; on Saturday morning it's twenty to twenty-five.

- According to a study cited by the American Psychological Association, TV contributes to sexual and racial stereotyping and aggressive behavior. All of this is sad when we consider that Americans don't take the impact of TV seriously.[46] We often fail to realize that what we watch often has a bearing on what we do. And many studies have shown that television violence encourages violent behavior.

- George Gerbner, dean emeritus of the Annenberg School for Communications suggests, "[TV] is contributing more than ever [to moral decisions]. The influence is pervasive." In addition to violence, television programs are filled with sex. Through 1991, according to one study, prime time shows on three networks depicted 10,218 sexual incidents—93 percent of them outside marriage.[47]

A Layering of Anti-Family Bias

How does all of this influence families and children? One observer gets to the core of the issue:

Before they reach the tender age of five, many children have mastered the controls of the television set, video recorder and Nintendo games in their homes. They have seen thousands of images race by, from Big Bird to multiple shootings to couples discussing sex on previews for 'L.A. Law.' The cumulative effect of this torrent of information and imagery is still being studied, but child psychologists warn that the very nature of the process may endanger children's healthy development. Most obviously, it cuts into time for other activities—when children are glued to the tube, they are not playing, reading or learning from adults. They are absorbing millions of images at an incredible rate, a process that has been cited as complicitous in the lowering of their attention spans and spawning a new generation of children weaned on and socialized by sound bites. Finally, and perhaps most dangerously, children are being exposed to an outpouring of materialism and to problems and dilemmas for which they may not be ready.[48]

Neil Postman argues that premature introduction of adult problems provokes anxiety in children and robs them of their innocence.[49] Bombarded with examples of every human foible, children begin to believe that the world around them is a far more dangerous, unstable place than it really is, and that anxiety is a normal state of mind.[50]

Psychologist David Elkind has observed that parents become hardened to the electronic outbursts in their living rooms. In time their resistance is dropped and parents become so accustomed to swearing, nudity, overt sexual activity, and violence on the screen, that they become less vigilant about what their children are watching.[51]

Some of the television that kids and their parents watch attack the family directly. Despite the values of the Cosby family, ". . . traditional male characteristics—such as independence, physical strength, daring, protectiveness, inventiveness, and authority—are cast in the darkest light. This development has followed the evolution of feminism, which began as a search for parity with men and became what media critic Martha Bayles calls the 'women are not only different—they're better' philosophy."[52]

A recent *Time* writer challenged the idea that television is harmful to families and argued instead that TV families are realistic and "at least stick together" despite their faults. He even suggests that, "The Simpsons, too, despite its 'eat my shorts' irreverence, presents a cohesive family that could almost be a role model."[53] I am being generous when I call such drivel a weak defense.

No One You'd Want to Know

Repeatedly, television depicts the American family in a precarious way. Consider, for example, one segment of *Married with Children*, in which Al Bundy arrives at his doorstep and proclaims, "Ah, home sweet hell." Upon arriving, he and his wife, Peg, have one of their normal conversations. "This is a home, not a restaurant," contends Peg after Al demands supper. Al comes back with, "I know, if it was a restaurant, we'd have a clean bathroom." Family values are scrapped in this sitcom.

Roseanne is another anti-family sitcom that retained its spot in the top prime time shows of 1992. Roseanne, the mother, is a working woman who complains constantly about her job, housework, and nagging kids. On one show she proclaims, "They're all mine. Of course, I'd trade any one of them for a dishwasher." The producer of *Roseanne*, Barbara Ehrenreich, suggests that the message of the show is that "Mom is no longer interested in being a human sacrifice on the altar of 'pro-family values.' "[54]

The depiction and treatment of issues on television is not always better. We have become accustomed to bite-sized information, and we accept media decisions about what is important enough to be on the public agenda. We forget that television primarily exists to entertain. Media people assume, probably correctly, that people get bored talking about one thing. We forget that history has often turned on one thing, like "The just shall live by faith alone," "No taxation without representation," or "A house divided against itself cannot stand." In contrast:

> Under the constant scrutiny of the media, we give a little attention to a lot of diverse issues. We are shown few connections. No coherent philosophy of life or government is allowed to emerge. Those who seek to provide a sense of priority are dismissed as single-issue zealots or hopelessly naive.[55]

Much of what I have said about the influence of television on our families applies as well to the movie-makers in Hollywood, the video tapes that get played in our living rooms, and the books and magazines that come into our homes. And much of what I have said is reinforced by the music that we hear on our stereos and that kids feed into their minds through their headphones.

It has been said that if you want to understand a culture you should listen to its music. In our society, music has shifted from Elvis, the Beatles, and Woodstock to today's discord of people like Ice-T singing about cop killing and Madonna's outrageous pornography in concerts and on MTV. Much of this is supplemented by Hollywood superstars and teenage idols whose lifestyles, words, and songs promote nonmarital and extramarital sexuality, cohabitation, children born out of wedlock, and other values that are hostile to the family.

Spiritual Warfare, Satan, and the Occult

Many years ago, C. S. Lewis wrote that one of Satan's most deceptive tactics is to convince people that he doesn't exist. Apparently he has done a good job in his deception. Most people think of the devil as no more than a symbol of evil: like Santa Claus, he is just a fictional symbol.[56]

A sizable minority of people, however, agree that Satan exists, just as the Bible says. From the beginning of the world, he has attacked marriages and sought to destroy families. He knows that the best way to devastate the world is to destroy relationships at their most basic level—in the home. As soon as sin entered the world, Satan began to attack marriage and tried to crush it because he knew that marriage was the foundation of right human relations.

In Genesis, the first book of the Bible, we read that Satan tried to corrupt God's design for marriage and family life by husband-wife tension (3:11–12), murderous sibling rivalry

(4:1–12), polygamy (4:19), adultery (16:1–3), homosexuality (19:4–11), fornication and rape (34:1, 2), incest (38:13–18), prostitution (38:24), evil seduction (39:7–12), and a variety of other tactics. We can see the efforts of the evil one throughout the Bible, and we can see this today.

"Satan knows that the best way to devastate the world is to destroy relationships at their most basic level—in the home."

I believe that Satan himself is the primary force behind every modern movement to destroy the children. When we offer condoms and birth control pills to middle schoolers and high schoolers, we are saying to them that adults approve of what they are doing and we deceive them into thinking that what they do can be done safely. This is Satanic because it ultimately destroys their bodies, their souls, and their spirit.

Abortion is a hellish doctrine that allows for total destruction of a generation of children. The use of drugs is clearly Satan's way of destroying the minds and bodies of our children. Free sex, anti-family values, and immorality are as old as Satan himself. We are in a spiritual warfare, and the church has the only answer for our society.

Fighting for the Family

Although much of the anti-family chaos in our society has been created in one generation, I believe that with the power of the Holy Spirit it also can be reversed in one generation. If this society and the families in it have any hope, that hope must come from Christian individuals and families and from pulpits where the Bible is respected and preached. Christian parents, Christian lay people, pastors, and all others who have an understanding of Judeo-Christian ethics must join forces to turn our society around.

Dr. Frances Schaeffer often spoke of "co-belligerents" working together for the greater good. In the cause of saving the family, I would hope that pro-family Catholics, mainline Protestants, evangelicals, charismatics, and others would join hands with secularists who may share our family values. Together we must reverse the anti-family trend and do it now.

Likewise, as we perform our "light of the world" ministry of changing a destructive anti-family trend, we must also perform our "salt of the earth" outreach. We must mobilize millions of pro-family Americans into an unbeatable voting bloc that will change the make-up of city councils, schools boards, State Legislatures, the Congress, the White House, and the Judicial system. We have the numbers and the power to do it.

This influence must be unified, mobilized, informed, and sent out. Parents and pastors must be the change agents who make all this happen. We must force governments to do what is right. We must shut down the anti-family voices on the left. We must outvote them. We must render them helpless and sterile. All of this will be difficult because the other side controls the media, dominates much of education, and wields significant political power.

Our crusade for the family must forget popularity polls. Christian leaders are called to be faithful not popular. We must ignore the national media since there is little hope in our generation of changing the wildly liberal and anti-family media in this country. We must run past them, around them, and over them. Again, we have the numbers and the influence to do it. What we need is blind courage and faith in the hearts of our pastors, parents, and everyone else who is dedicated to the family. If we do this, we can change the minds of the politicians, the textbooks, and the curricula of our schools. But our time is running out. We must do it now!

6

OUR EMOTIONAL DEMISE

I n a world in which family values have been reduced to a matter of mere convenience, loneliness and depression will rise. By their very nature, people need love on a long-term basis; without concerned and caring attachments, they will be confronted by difficult, often shattering, emotional struggles. Today these conditions are epidemic in this country. The cheapening of relationships by a slick, fast-paced, devil-may-care secular society, and the justification of easy-sex without commitments, has created a tidal wave of broken families and wounded spirits.

Children of Divorce

Divorce, the most visible sign of a culture in collapse, has become easy in our society. For many, divorce seems a relatively simple solution to a complex problem, a cheap way to escape from a troublesome marriage. Almost all experts agree, however, that divorce puts enormous strain on everybody involved, and the ones who pay the greatest price are usually the children. Over a million children begin paying that price every single year in the United States: a total of more than twenty million since 1972.[1]

Many couples do not realize how profoundly the lives of their children are affected by their marital problems. Even young children know about separation and divorce. They hear about their friends' parents who have separated, and they worry about the stability of their own families. It is no longer rare for even small children to ask plaintive questions such as, "Daddy, are you and Mommy going to get a divorce?"

When parents divorce, children must adapt to the separation from one parent and the establishment of a new relationship with the other. Children naturally feel uncomfortable having to choose one parent over another, and they often feel they must learn how to appease both. In some cases, this means living with two sets of values, or never mentioning one parent in the presence of the other.

In addition, young victims of divorce have to change schools, friends, and familiar surroundings at a time in their lives when they most need stability. Almost always, parental separations and divorce bring tension, stress, and devastating hardships.

Psychologist Judith S. Wallerstein astonished many readers with her book which confirmed the pain that is experienced by many children when their parents separate. The research showed that children of divorce are frequently very angry and feel lost in all the shuffle.[2]

Among the researchers' findings are the facts that very young children fear abandonment, and children of all ages tend to feel guilt that their own behavior might have caused their parents' breakup. In other cases, children feel that they are being forced to pay for their parents' mistakes.

Many of these children suffer severe emotional problems, such as anxiety, insecurity, and discouragement, and these are not just temporary problems. In many cases, they will last for years after their parents separate—sometimes the rest of their lives. Such emotions can continue undetected in single-parent families even if the parent is deeply devoted to his or her children.

Children of divorce have to struggle to adjust, and sometimes this causes behavioral problems. It may come as a surprise that the youngest children have the greatest difficulty adjusting, for at this very young age, they are incapable of understanding why their family is breaking up. Somehow the words, "Mommy and Daddy just can't get along," do not seem adequate. Consequently, some children develop a fear of being abandoned which may haunt them forever. In their effort to cope, sometimes older boys have a tendency to behave aggressively, and some research suggests they are more prone to use alcohol and drugs.[3]

Girls appear to be more resilient, at least on the surface, but they suffer longer-term effects that include feelings of anxiety and difficulties in relating to the opposite sex as they get older. Even college-age and adult children are torn when their parents divorce. Some say that the discovery that "Mom and Dad never liked each other" can be shattering. These facts are overwhelming. When marriages break up, kids suffer. And the suffering is often accentuated by the strain of living in a single-parent family.

Another Look at Single Parents

The *Wall Street Journal* recently published a thought-provoking article about one-parent families. It reported that more than half the black children, about one-third of Hispanic kids, and almost one in five white children now live in single-parent homes—percentages that parallel the percentages of children in these groups who live in poverty. A majority of these children live with mothers who often struggle financially, and more and more fathers simply disappear, refusing to support their children after the divorce.[4]

Many fathers leave without agreeing to pay child support, and of those who do agree, more than half never fully comply. A lot of fathers apparently regard marriage as a "package deal"—when they divorce their wives, they divorce the kids as well. Among those who do give financial support, the level is often so low that it doesn't really help, and the single mom and her kids end up on the verge of poverty.[5]

The *Wall Street Journal* article mentioned above also referred to a major research study that apparently reached some relatively conservative conclusions. Even though published by the liberal Annie E. Casey Foundation and Center for the Study of Social Policy, the study showed that breaking up a marriage causes many long-term problems for children.

For years, the report said, evidence has shown that living in a single-parent family has been associated with childhood problems including poor health, stunted physical growth, higher rates of delinquency, and difficulties in school. Low grades and lower reading skills are observed, along with poor spelling and math scores.[6]

Perhaps it is not surprising that children from single-parent homes also have increased levels of stress, depression, anxiety, aggression, early sexual experience, mental illness, substance abuse, juvenile delinquency, youth gang membership, and other physical, emotional, and behavioral problems.[7]

Many liberal commentators have tried to explain away this data by arguing that the problems of single-parent families come from economic disadvantage, racial discrimination, or the failure of government to provide adequate welfare benefits. Eliminate these, they say, and family welfare would improve, regardless of the types of homes in which kids live. But the Casey Foundation report challenges this kind of thinking. It breaks with the widely held view that any living arrangement called a family is a suitable place to raise children. Instead, the report likens the single-parent family to calamities such as infant mortality or violent teen-age deaths, and it presents facts that are devastating to those who argue that one kind of family is as good for children as another.

The *Wall Street Journal* article concludes with some sobering words:

> If we want to get serious about the rising number of children who are coming into society ill-fed, ill-housed, ill-educated, and ill-cared for, we will have to confront more than these symptoms of family breakdown. We will have to develop strategies, involving both public and private resources, that succeed not just in caring for single-parent families, but in diminishing their number.[8]

I admire those women and men who work hard to make ends meet and to raise their kids as best they can without a partner. Those who have not been through it, including myself, will never really understand just how hard it is. But despite many heroic efforts by concerned single parents, children from these homes usually get less parental attention, less affection and supervision, and less confidence in their own worth and personal security than children in two-parent families.

Even when there is a strong devotion to their children, single parents have to work long hours to care for family needs. Frequently, money is in short supply and the overburdened parent lacks the time or energy for quality interactions with the children. Loneliness, isolation, and depression in these children is inevitable, and these conditions can be even worse if there are persisting tensions between the divorced or divorcing parents.[9] Any way you look at it, children in single-parent families have an enormous disadvantage.

Growing Up with Drugs or Alcohol at Home

One of the newer areas of research for psychologists in recent years is the set of problems associated with "adult children of alcoholics" (ACOA). Today millions of people have grown up in homes where one or both parents were alcoholic. Counselors and members of ACOA groups around the nation agree that living with an alcoholic parent can have devastating effects, many of which do not even surface until years afterward. Even after becoming adults and leaving home, adult children of alcoholics bear deep emotional scars from their painful past experiences.

If these independent adults bear scars, the effects on dependent children can be traumatic. There are individual differences, of course, but when compared to children from non-alcoholic families, kids with alcoholic parents have more physical problems than kids from non-alcoholic homes (including headaches, stomachaches, tiredness, sleep disturbances, fear, sadness, embarrassment, difficulty getting along with other kids, and a variety of academic and behavioral problems).[10]

Many of these children do not have their physical or psychological needs met in the family. A child's needs for love, belonging, and security cannot be met by parents who have lost control over their lives and who often dislike themselves because of their own drinking behavior. Children in alcoholic homes often have low self-esteem, and many are angry and hostile toward their parents. As these children grow older, they are frequently involved in delinquency or other antisocial behaviors; and often these young people end up abusing alcohol themselves—despite a frequent determination not to become like their parents.

Preachers used to pound their pulpits and recite the evils of drunkenness for congregations of church members who didn't drink. Today, drinking has become common, even among many Christians. Television commericals that portray the joys of drinking are all around us, and many churches seem to have forgotten the Bible's teaching that alcohol is a mocker and the person who is deceived by it is not wise (Proverbs 20:1).

The effects of alcohol abuse have ruined millions of lives, including the lives of children. In addition, today we are faced with a drug epidemic that is compounding the problems, even in preschool children. A recent report by the Child Welfare League reveals that there is an increase in the number of families seeking help for alcohol and drug abuse in preschool children who now show behavioral and developmental problems from being exposed to alcohol and drugs before birth.[11]

Considering the number of new babies that have been exposed to illegal drugs in the womb (a reported 15 percent), it is easy to agree with those who say that we are in the midst of a major drug-related crisis that has direct and devastating impact on the American family.

Who Is Minding the Kids?

Since the economy frequently requires that both mother and father be in the work force, children are often left at home unattended while their parents work. These "latch-key kids" lock the house in the mornings and unlock the house when they come home from school in the afternoon with no adult in attendance.

Some authorities suggest that 15 to 20 percent of early elementary school children and approximately 45 percent of late-elementary schoolchildren are unsupervised for some part of the day.[12]

Although many of these kids are ignored by their parents, often families are deeply concerned. Dual-income middle class families find good quality care for their children difficult to locate, but for parents with lower incomes the task is almost impossible. Some businesses are trying to help and so are a host of community child care facilities, but for a lot of kids, part of every day is spent by themselves at home.

How do latch-key children react? Many are scared, and evidence suggests that many exhibit feelings of intense anxiety, loneliness, boredom, and worry. While unsupervised, these children tend to spend too many hours watching television, snacking improperly, ignoring exercise, and delaying homework and chores till late in the evening. Some of them become "couch potatoes" while they are still little kids.

Things don't always get better when the parents come home. After working all day, and faced with household chores that need to be done on weekends or in the evening, many parents are too tired, too irritable, or too pressured to spend time with their children. As a result, the children remain starved for the love and attention they need and often crave.

Growing Up Homeless

Some families these days don't have to worry about abuse in the home, divorce, substance abuse, or latch-key children— these families are homeless. Nobody can estimate the numbers accurately, but some suggest that the oft-cited figure of 3 million is probably low. For years derelicts and alcoholics have walked the streets of our inner cities, but today there is a whole new look and feel to the problem of homelessness.

"Young boys and girls are being loaded down with problems and insecurities with which no child is prepared to cope."

Some of the estimates I have seen suggest that more than a third of all homeless people are in families that have children; and roughly half of these are headed by single women between the ages of seventeen and twenty-five. Many have never married or are separated or divorced. Most are high school graduates, many have attended college, and often they are people who want jobs, homes, family life, and stable incomes, but they simply can't find work. Unlike those hard core families who seem to be quite satisfied to subsist on government assistance, many of the new homeless are eager to work, but they cannot find jobs or day care while they look for a job.

How are these homeless children affected by their circumstances? The truth is, no one knows; but certainly they are faced with serious problems. What other people take for granted—a place to call home—these children wonder and worry about. Many are anxious about food, safety, shelter, a place to call their own, or even whether or not they will survive. Their future is a serious concern. They worry about their parents, and typically they are undernourished, under-developed, and undereducated.[13]

Perhaps these are the greatest victims of the spiritual emptiness, misplaced values, and bankrupt social philosophies that abound in our society and that play havoc with family life. Young boys and girls are being loaded down with problems and insecurities with which no child is prepared to cope.

Anti-Family Influences on the Individual

It is easy enough to talk about the ways that our nation is influenced by the value vacuum in our society. We can read, too, about broken marriages and struggling children without being greatly affected if we feel our own marriages are intact and our kids seem to be surviving. But the problems that undermine countries, marriages, and children can hit any one of us today. No one is ultimately secure in such a climate. One Christian psychologist suggests that, in one way or another, we are all victims, though some of us don't know it yet.

Consider, for example, how our shifting values have left millions of Americans confused about what they believe or why. For centuries, most people learned their values from their parents, teachers, or churches, and most shared similar ideas about what is good or bad, right or wrong. But within recent years we have gone through what has been called a "values revolution" so that many people have no idea where they stand on anything.

A whole generation claims to have minds that are open to all people, all viewpoints, all religions, all ideas, and all lifestyle preferences. Tolerance and openness are lauded; having firm beliefs is considered old-fashioned and out of touch with reality. But is that really the case?

As Professor Allan Bloom has argued, the same minds that claim to be open to everything are really ignorant of the great thinking of the past. They have substituted easy pleasure and "creature comforts" for intellectual industry, and as a result they tend to be intellectually lazy and unwilling to entertain the idea that some conclusions are better than others. They live in a quagmire of "moral equivalence," where everything is equal and no values are considered superior. Is it really surprising in such a world then, that millions of people feel that they are drifting, with no absolute values or beliefs to which they can anchor their lives?[14]

So many people today feel empty inside, without standards of right and wrong, and with no guidelines for raising children, maintaining a marriage, building careers, doing business, or knowing God. Now, perhaps more than at any time in history, people are looking for truth, for identity, for something to believe in. They need truths that will give their lives a real center.[15]

Floundering in the midst of "values relativity," great numbers of Americans today have lives that are marked by meaninglessness, loneliness, loss of self-control, guilt, and anger.

Meaninglessness

Several years ago, Francis Schaeffer wrote that many people make decisions based on "pragmatism," the idea elaborated by philosopher William James that if something works then it must be right. If that is the only standard, then people begin to make decisions based on what will bring "personal peace and comfort." Beyond that there are few standards.

If Schaeffer was right, and I believe he was, then we should have expected the avalanche of meaninglessness that has fallen upon the land. When we have no reason for living, apart from our own hedonistic gratification, then it is not long before we feel empty, anxious, and rootless. Many would agree with psychiatrist Viktor Frankl who wrote that meaninglessness is the root cause of depression, addictions, and aggression—all of which are highly prevalent in America today.

As we look briefly at each of these emotional problems, we can see the statistics. There are estimates that thirty to forty million people in the United States are affected, at least periodically, by chronic *depresssion*.[16] In the course of a lifetime, one in four women and one in ten men in the United States can expect to experience a major depression.

In another insightful article, psychologist Martin Seligman compared depression among baby boomers with their parents and grandparents. He found that people in the baby boom generation are about ten times more likely to be depressed as young adults. Although they pretend to be optimistic, thousands of baby boomers are sliding into melancholy, in part because of unfulfilled expectations and lives that are empty and meaningless.

Past generations were able to maintain hope through difficult times because they had three anchors of stability: faith in God, pride in one's country, and stability in the family. All three of these anchors seem to have disintegrated during the baby boom decades, and an upsurge of depression has been the result.[17]

Concerning *addictions*, we know that alcohol tops the list of drugs that are used and abused by Americans. Studies show that from 70 to 93 percent of adults drink alcohol in this country and that one out of every ten adults is an alcoholic.[18] Government research estimates that 70 percent of Americans use alcohol. The higher figure of 93 percent refers to those who "use or have used" alcohol.[19]

An estimated eighteen million Americans over the age of eighteen experience problems related to alcohol; this includes five million women who experience alcohol-related problems. Of these, less than 20 percent will ever get treatment.

"Past generations were able to maintain hope through difficult times because they had three anchors of stability: faith in God, pride in one's country, and stability in the family."

The story is hardly any better when we look at the statistics concerning those who abuse drugs other than alcohol. The National Institute on Drug Abuse estimates that twenty-three million Americans over the age of twelve have at some time used illegal drugs.[20] Of these, less than 2 percent use narcotics such as heroin, but 13 percent of young adults and 17 percent of older adults have used or are using hallucinogens, such as LSD or PCP; and 19 percent of young adults and 26 percent of older adults use or are using cocaine or crack.

As we turn to *aggression,* the third of the three results of meaninglessness observed by Viktor Frankl, we are confronted with the specter of rising violence, including violence in the home. Reportedly, one out of every four homes was affected in some way by violence during a recent year, and police departments around the country confirm that the problems are getting worse, not better. This also includes violence against one's self, represented by suicide. Suicide is a serious problem in all sectors of society today, but among children and teenagers, suicide is the second leading cause of death, after accidents.

All of this has been summarized in a few words by Christian counselor Paul Welter. Since they lack meaning and have nothing to live for, "millions of despairing people are retreating from life through the avenue of depression, reaching for excitement through addictions and seeking power through violence."[21]

Loneliness

God knew that it was not good for individuals to be alone. So he created a companion for Adam and gave men and women the need for fellowship and a desire for family life. Today, however, many are still lonely. Roughly one out of every four adults in our society lives alone and these numbers are expected to reach 33 percent by the year 2000.[22] Some are elderly and confined to solitary rooms because they can't get around independently, or they are too afraid to go out. Others are younger but unable to develop or maintain close relationships.

When people lack close and meaningful relationships with others, they tend to feel restless, anxious, empty, and discouraged, even when they are surrounded by other people. Many years ago, Paul Tournier wrote a thoughtful book on loneliness and concluded that,

> People are lonely because a spirit of competitiveness pervades our culture. People demand independence, the freedom to live their own life. They seek happiness as if it were something to be owned. They demand justice, equality, and rights. Yet they misunderstand their deepest needs. Instead of competitiveness,

they need community; instead of independence, cooperation; instead of possessing happiness, sharing happiness; and instead of rights, love. In short, the answer to loneliness is community and love.[23]

Loneliness is the painful realization that we lack close and meaningful contact with others. Often loneliness is the price tag for being "personally liberated," highly ambitious, and on the "fast track." Consumed with activities and business, people get lost in their pursuits and miss the essence of personal intimacy and family togetherness. Many work in crowded cities and interact with people all day, but they feel intense loneliness inside. It is little wonder that so many people desperately want to "slow down" and find greater stability. Some are beginning to search for the freedom from loneliness that can only be found in the confines of the family and in traditional "family values."

Guilt

Counselors hear some of the same phrases over and over again: "getting over it," "recovery," "unfinished business," "dealing with the past," "handling my guilt." These phrases have something in common. They all point to a desire to get free of the addictions, bitterness, painful experiences, and memories that come from the past. In counseling, people want to get beyond the scars and suffering from the past and move more freely into the future. To do that, people often have to get disentangled from their feelings of guilt.

The drug use, sexual promiscuity, unfaithfulness, rebellion, pushing for personal fulfillment, broken relationships, and unkept promises of the last thirty years have left many feeling shame and remorse.

Such emotions can lead to many kinds of behavior which produce guilt. We all know about drug and alcohol addictions, but millions of people have addictions of a different kind. They are addicted to food, exercise, power, pornography, television, sports, career-building, work, or sex, to name a few. Addictions are compulsive actions that control us so much that we persist in the addictive behavior, even if this hurts others or ourselves.

Although they often become tied to our physiology, such addictions are, in fact, selfish and totally self-centered. Our addictions eventually control us; while they may bring temporary periods of pleasure, they are ultimately self-destructive. Even though addictions are harmful, the addict concludes that "I must have this or do this in order to be OK." This is the root of addictive disorders.

Most of us know people who are work addicts. They work all the time, explain away their workaholism, and refuse to admit that their behavior could destroy themselves or their families.

Less visible are sexual addictions, those "secret sins" that control as many as 10 percent of the Christian population, and probably greater numbers of people outside the church.[24] These individuals, often fathers and mothers, substitute deviant and unhealthy sexual patterns in place of marital intimacy, commitment, and other healthy sexual behaviors.

Many of these sexually-addicted people grew up in dysfunctional, unhealthy families. Some may have been abused sexually. Many have no understanding of what healthy sexuality is all about, so they become obsessed and preoccupied with sex. Almost everything in life—their plans, thoughts, habits, mannerisms, language—all are related to sex.[25]

As time passes, the addiction exerts greater and greater control over their lives. Eventually, even the guilt that was there at the beginning begins to wane and the individual feels hopelessly trapped. Imagine how addictions like this could tear apart families, destroy careers, and turn churches upside down if the addicted person should be a Christian leader.

As we move toward the next century, we no longer will be able to ignore the consequences of our lack of self-control, immorality, self-centered lifestyles, and addictive behaviors. Combined with despair and loneliness, guilt will continue to bind millions of people who are having to face the consequences of their own selfish activities.

Guilt is a moral issue, and guilt feelings result from moral failures. But feeling guilty over our failures is really a starting point for positive change. Social programs can help to bring change in the society, but the personal pain, sorrow, and guilt that we feel because of our decadency and irresponsibility will not go away in response to anything that we might do. Instead, we must admit our failures and turn to a heavenly Father who is loving, willing to forgive, and able to help us deal with the guilt that holds sway over so many lives.

Where Do We Go from Here?

I believe that the happiest people on the face of this earth are those who are part of great homes and families where they are loved, protected, and shielded. When I have been out having a long, hard day, often in a hostile environment, it is great to walk into my home, close the front door, and know that inside there are the people I love and who love me in return.

For me, home is a haven to which I run from the troubles of this world, a place of security and warmth, where each member belongs and knows it. Ideally, a home is a place where there are conversations around the dinner table about the days events. A family is a place where people can be real with each other, laughing together, sharing hurts, and having their tears wiped away. Home is where people assure each other with support and give one another encouragement and love.

Is that an idealistic picture? Maybe. For the past two chapters we have looked at overwhelming evidence showing that most homes fall far short of the ideal. There seem to be fewer and fewer stable homes. As we have seen, huge numbers of people live in families where mothers and father hate each other and where children live in perpetual fear and uncertainty. Many of those who lead the anti-family efforts in America are bitter because of their own failures in their families. They are steeped in the tragic fallout of dysfunctional families and are not able to see that families could be different.

A commentator from one of the major networks once asked, "What right do you Baptists have to promote your ideas about the family being the acceptable style for all of humanity?" I replied that it was not Baptists who started the family; it was God Almighty, and He is not a Baptist.

God established the husband-wife relationship and instructed us to multiply and control and contain the earth. God respected women and children, even as He gave fathers the special responsibility of guiding the family and of consistently living a good lifestyle before his family. The father is to pray with his family and for them, and he must bring up his children in accordance with the Word of God. Nobody can do these things unless that person knows Jesus Christ as Lord and Savior.

God is not in the business of squelching our needs, degrading women, or making our lives miserable. But until individuals are in a right relationship with God, there is no hope for righting our families. Because we have weak and sometimes absent parents, including weak fathers who have ignored their families, we also have weak families and children who probably will grow up to become weak parents themselves, leading even weaker homes.

"Until individuals are in a right relationship with God, there is no hope for righting our families."

This does not need to happen. God has a plan for the family. It is a plan that can be a foundation for rebuilding families that are stable and functional, even in these times of change and turmoil. But before we can live in the bounty and beauty of that plan, we must overcome the anti-family values of the surrounding world which threaten us today.

Before turning to a fuller discussion of God's plan for the family, I think it is important to examine the ways in which the secular anti-family agenda threatens the hopes of families. That will be the subject of the following chapter.

7

ASSESSING
THE DAMAGE

T he family is the foundational building block of society, and its health is a prerequisite for a healthy and prosperous nation. No nation has ever been stronger than its families.

With our widespread rejection of the historic faith of our fathers, however, and because of a loss of commitment to family, we are beginning to see the erosion of America's stability as a nation. Never before has the American family been in so much trouble. The wounds run deep and the costs are high. We are faced with a shaky economy, devastating poverty, rising homelessness, problems with our public health system, the deterioration of public education even as the schools increasingly seek to give their own secular values to our kids. We have frightening dilemmas in mental health care in this country and widespread devaluation of the work ethic.

The dissolution of ethical absolutes and "family values" escalates the dangers of crime and social dysfunction at an alarming rate. Violent crimes, for example, rose 10 percent in 1990. This country now has the highest incarceration rate among all nations with nearly a million men, women, and young people behind bars.[1] Alcoholism remains a national scandal. One recent survey indicates that there are more than eleven million alcoholics in the United States, and seventy-six million families are touched in some way by alcohol abuse. In 1986, alcohol and its effects cost the people of this country $128.3 billion.[2]

Drug use and addiction are an ongoing problem. During one recent year, more than 14 percent of the population, age twelve and older (a total of twenty-eight million), had used illicit drugs, including marijuana, cocaine, inhalants, hallucinogens, heroin, and the non-medical use of psychotherapeutic drugs. Over 7 percent of the population (14.5 million) were current users.[3]

Our children are also struggling. Those under sixteen make up the largest group of Americans without health insurance. The mortality rate for children in the U.S. is one of the highest among industrialized nations. In addition, more than half of all white children and 76 percent of African-American children will spend part of their childhood in a single parent home.

On top of that, nearly ninety kids a day are taken from their parents by government agents. Every day over five hundred children between the ages of ten and fourteen begin using illegal drugs, and one thousand start drinking alcohol.[4]

In the schools, children are being taught that it is wrong to be "homophobic" but all right to be homosexual.[5] Students soon learn that "accepting homosexuality is more important than learning the three R's."[6]

The number of teen pregnancies and abortions are also at epidemic proportions. The United States has the highest rate of unmarried teen pregnancies, births, and abortions among the developed countries of the world, with over one million teen pregnancies and over 400,000 abortions each year.[7]

Assessing the Damage

When I stop to survey the wreckage of American society brought about by three decades of hedonistic, godless social programming, I am stunned and heartbroken. I can only agree with Chuck Colson and Jack Eckerd who have written that:

> The breakdown of family life has an immediate effect on our children, since it is in families that human beings learn manners, hygiene, speech, discipline, morality, values, and the importance of getting and holding a job. Once the cycle of dependency has begun each generation sinks deeper into despair and hopelessness.[8]

It is difficult to stop and difficult to break.

Sadly, we have become a society of victims, with everybody accusing someone else for their problems. To get privileges you have to have "victim" status; you have to be exploited, abused, neglected, insulted, or slurred to get attention. Rather than seeking recovery, millions are racing to claim their rights as victims or an abused minority of some type.

This has made us, at the same time, a nation of blamers, always looking for somebody else to criticize and accuse. When we spend time blaming one another, nobody owns the problems and nobody takes responsibility for doing anything about the situation. This is especially true if we put the blame on something vague like "society," "education," or "the government." How often have you seen President George Bush attacked for everything that goes wrong in America. It seemed to me that the editors of *Newsweek* even did their best to blame the president for hurricane Andrew!

No great society can survive with such attitudes. Instead, we must all take ownership and responsibility for bringing about positive change. It is time for morally sensitive people to stand and defend our heritage. Issues that have to do with the very health and future stability of this republic and her families need to be dealt with honestly and openly by people who care. That should include every American citizen. If everyone contributes to the solutions, we can all share the credit and the blame equally. The greatest shame is to do nothing at all, then criticize those who tried their best.

I am convinced that the starting place for revitalization in this country is with a renewal of our spiritual heritage. In Proverbs, Solomon wrote, "Righteousness exalts a nation, but sin is a reproach to any people" (Proverbs 14:34). The strength of America and our families has been in our right-eousness, in our walk. But today many in our nation have dismissed the value of religion altogether.

When religion ceases to be a major force in any society—as Arnold Toynbee argued convincingly in his classic, *A Study of History*—nations perish. Already the moral fiber of this country is weakening, in part, because we have ignored God and pursued or tolerated selfish lusts that bring tempo-rary pleasure. The problems of ethical collapse are so perva-sive that it doesn't take a theologian to spot it. Every news magazine and editorial commentator has voiced concern and outrage at these conditions.

In recent years, sin and immorality often seem to be the national pastime, but they offer a pleasure that fades quickly (Hebrews 11:25). The God who is loving, compassionate, and forgiving is also a God of judgment; He will not tolerate our immorality forever. It is tragic that we are hastening His judgment and our own destruction by turning away from

God, tearing apart the family, and ultimately destroying our culture from within.

According to the Bible, marriage is a sacred bond in which the man and woman leave their parents, come together as husband and wife, and unite with one another in partnership and intimacy that lasts for a lifetime. To become one, each gives up his or her right to independence; they become life partners, working for a common goal and sense of unity. By no means does this suggest that they have to squelch their personalities or ignore problems when they arise. Instead, husband and wife commit themselves to live, work, and grow together, bonded by their commitment to one another and to God.

This, of course, is a fantasy in the lives of many couples, especially to those who skip the wedding. In fact, more than half of all people now in their thirties are estimated to have lived in a cohabiting relationship, and roughly half of all recent marriages were preceded by cohabitation.[9]

Within the past two decades, there has been a significant increase in the number of unmarried couple households. Government figures may be a little deceptive—since they may also include adult roommates living in the same apartment—but between 1970 and 1988, the total number of unmarried couple households rose from 523,000 to 2,588,000.[10] Undoubtedly most of these are cohabiting couples.

Although this type of living arrangement was once considered to be morally reprehensible, it has become common in just the past few years. The same research cited above shows that among young adults today, only one in five disapproves of premarital sex, and no more than one in six explicitly disapprove of cohabitation.[11]

Surely much of the increase in unmarried couple households comes because of the increase in sexual freedom among adolescents and unmarried adults. But cohabitation also seems related to the values and experiences of the baby boomers who have now reached adulthood. When they were younger, many of these couples watched their parents' marriages disintegrate. Many come from broken homes; in addition, they have seen divorce happen to their friends.

In their desire to prevent this from happening in their own lives, some couples apparently "try out" marriage by living together before making a "long-term marriage commitment." Of singles who expect to cohabit in the future, more than 80 percent say they think the "trial marriage" is an important reason for cohabitation. While 40 percent of cohabiting couples eventually split up (the average time together is about eighteen months), a slightly greater number actually do get married. But research shows that these marriages are *less* stable than marriages that were formed without prior cohabitation.

Psychologist David Myers found this in his study of what makes people happy. A majority of the college students surveyed agreed that a couple should live together before marriage, but he wanted to find out what happens when these unions lead to marriage? According to Myers, seven recent studies concur that, compared to couples who don't cohabit with their spouses-to-be, those who do have *higher* divorce rates.[12]

Three national surveys illustrate this: a U.S. survey of thirteen thousand adults found that couples who lived together before marriage were one-third more likely to separate or divorce within a decade. A 1990 Gallup survey of still-married Americans also found that 40 percent of those who had cohabited before marrying, and 21 percent of those who had not, said they might divorce.

A Canadian national survey of fifty-three hundred women found that those who cohabited were 54 percent more likely to divorce within fifteen years. And a Swedish study of forty-three hundred women found cohabitation linked with an 80 percent greater risk of divorce.

"People who cohabit before marriage have less stable marriages and a far greater likelihood of divorce—with all the pain and sorrow it brings to everybody involved."

"Successful trial marriages do *not* predict a successful marriage," the researcher concludes. Some people may view cohabitation as little more than an "alternative lifestyle," but the effects of this lifestyle on later marriages can be devastating. To me these data appear to be overwhelming. People who cohabit before marriage have less stable marriages and a far greater likelihood of divorce—with all the pain and sorrow it brings to everybody involved.

Whatever Happened to Commitment?

Commitment is the foundation of a stable marriage. This may seem a revolutionary idea to anyone who has grown up in this age of individualism and personal fulfillment, when relationships are often short-lived. But when the permanence of the marriage relationship is not valued, divorce is more prevalent and genuine intimacy is far less likely.[13]

Studies of good, solid marriages show that they all begin with the husband and wife having a deep commitment to each other and to their marriage vows. Based on his studies of strong families, psychologist and researcher George Rekers concluded that members of such families place a high priority on family life. Typically, a high level of commitment begins in the married couple's relationship, when the husband and wife view their solemn pledge of marriage as a lifelong commitment to one another "for better or for worse."[14]

Mark Twain might have been right when he said that "No man or woman really knows what perfect love is until they have been married a quarter of a century." Indeed, that's commitment.

When a husband and wife are committed to their marriage and to each other, their attitudes spill over into the relationship between parents and kids. The children in families marked by commitment feel greater stability and security. They live in homes where there tend to be more of those character-building interactions that enable children to develop more smoothly into mature human beings.

This complex growth process is aided considerably when the parents are present, physically and emotionally, and when they make a lifelong commitment to each other.[15]

When commitment is lacking in a marriage, the next generation is more likely to conclude that divorce is acceptable, and that putting effort into making your marriage work need not be a high priority. With such assumptions, the seeds of destruction are sown from the very start.

Of course all marriages have problems, some of which come from the pressure-packed society in which we live. That doesn't surprise anyone. But when the inevitable problems get progressively worse and threaten to undermine a marriage, there can be dismay, disappointment, deep discouragement, and all too often a decision to end it. When separation and divorce do occur, intense psychological pain, spiritual emptiness, feelings of insecurity, and a tremendous sense of failure result.[16] Commitment doesn't always prevent divorce, but it goes a long way toward keeping families together—helping them avoid the life turmoil and disruption that almost always follow when marriages crumble.

Are We Too Distracted to Communicate?

In recent years the term "couch potato" has been used to describe those people who race home from work to tune in the TV and tune out the family. Such people can sit for hours, glued to their chair in front of the television set, without any effort to interact with the people around them. They don't communicate well. They don't participate in what's going on. Often they don't have the time and frequently they don't make the effort. They are not members of a family; they are more like zombies, and hardly better than vegetables!

These people remind me of the story told many years ago by Swiss counselor Paul Tournier. He once met a surgeon whose life was completely taken up by his work. The man's wife felt neglected so she consulted a psychiatrist who recommended that the couple take at least one evening a week to spend time together. The surgeon was willing to cooperate, so every Friday evening he took his wife to a movie where they watched the film and then went home.

With this weekly ritual completed, the doctor felt less guilty about his workaholism, so he went back to work. It was a step in the right direction, Tournier wrote, but the relationship remained strained because there was little communication and no effort to understand each other.[17]

With all the pressures facing couples and families today, it is not surprising that we have so many people who are too busy or too tired to communicate with one another. How can a couple learn to care for each other when they are too busy with personal pursuits? How can they be united as "one" when they are totally occupied by the distractions of this fast-changing society?

Communication, like commitment, is one of the building blocks of a strong marriage. It should come as no surprise that good communication is also a mark of strong families. Unlike troubled marriages, where poor communication is always present, good marriages and strong families are made up of people who are good communicators. They respect one another and are skilled in expressing their thoughts, desires, and emotions.

Good communication like this does not come automatically, however. We need to work on communicating, both with our spouses and with the other members of our families. And we need to recognize that effective communication involves both verbal (what we say with our mouths) and nonverbal messages (what we say with our actions or voice inflections).

Effective communication also involves listening. When family members are too busy or too distracted to listen, communication breakdown is inevitable. Sometimes spouses or family members listen halfheartedly, and this contributes to miscommunication. Usually people feel unheard or ignored if there is only partial listening. People have become so busy with their careers that they fail to listen or communicate, and today we live in an information age with even greater distractions and a greater likelihood of communication breakdowns and subsequent marriage failures. It takes time to communicate clearly, but nothing is more important to a wholesome family relationship.

What About Infidelity?

It is ironic that some people who do not have time for building their marriage relationships seem to have plenty of time for sex outside marriage. That, at least, is what we must conclude from the reports of marital infidelity in our country. Couples make a vow of fidelity at the altar, and many would agree with the Bible's clear statements that adultery is sin (Exodus 20:14; Matthew 5:27, 28). However, infidelity today is soaring to unprecedented heights.[18]

A recent national survey discovered that nearly 31 percent of all married Americans have had or are now having an affair. Almost two-thirds of these people don't think there is anything wrong with their actions.[19] Other studies indicate that 50 to 65 percent of all married men and 45 to 55 percent of all married women have had at least one extramarital experience by the time they reach age forty.[20]

Psychologist Henry Virkler recently wrote an entire book on infidelity and concluded that this can be one of the most painful and devastating experiences that a married person can ever encounter. It destroys trust and fuels the fires of both doubt and fear. Often it leaves the perpetrator feeling guilty and the victim feeling like a failure who was forsaken for another sexual partner. Infidelity frequently leaves lasting memories and deep insecurities in the minds of those who are affected.[21]

There are no simple explanations as to why supposedly solid marriages can fall subject to affairs. In part, however, the problems come because marriages often lack true intimacy. With idealistic expectations for one's marriage and sometimes with little awareness of the dangers of sexual temptation, some couples begin marriage buoyed by the joys of marital bliss. When the initial excitement fades, the marriage seems empty because there is little commitment to building a lasting relationship based on unconditional love.

It is tragic that infidelity and a lifestyle of casual sex are glorified in day-time television and other media. This philosophy tells men and women that they do not have to be committed to a marriage partner or to their children, but that they should be free to express their sexual urges whenever there is an opportunity.

Sexual promiscuity has become the lifestyle of America. This cult of sensualism is more than a revolution of dirty magazines and sexually explicit motion pictures. Infidelity and marital infidelity represent a pervasive lifestyle that always corrupts the family. Men and women who indulge in such practices knowingly sacrifice their own families to gratify their sexual desire.

This kind of lifestyle also leads to the destruction of careers, inner peace, and sometimes even lives. "The biggest mistake I ever made in my life was to leave your mother for another woman," a middle-age father recently wrote to his teenage son. The man who wrote this note took his own life after his relationship and his career had fallen apart.

Home Sweet Home Is Sometimes Dangerous

From time to time we hear about somebody whose seemingly good marriage has fallen apart. Our surprise turns to shock and sadness if we also learn that abuse or adultery has been a problem in the home for many years. But such cases are no longer rare, even in Christian homes.

Generally in such cases the husband is the abuser, but there is an increasing incidence of cases in which women are guilty of abuse. The reasons are complex in both cases, but often the abusive person uses violence (or the threat of violence) to gain control. Abuse occurs in the households of both married and cohabiting couples, and it tends to take on three forms: physical abuse, sexual abuse, and psychological abuse (involving actions such as rejection, constant verbal criticism, demeaning comments, or even ignoring one's mate completely).

The statistics of abuse are staggering and the effects are often overwhelming. One study estimated that approximately 3.5 million women and 250,000 men in the United States have been battered by a spouse or intimate partner.[22] According to other research, 25 to 30 percent of all American women are beaten at least once in the course of intimate relationships.[23]

FBI reports indicate that 30 percent of the women who were murdered in this country during one recent year were killed by their husbands or boyfriends.[24] These figures cannot begin to convey the terror, physical and emotional pain, and shattered self-esteem that accompany abusive behavior.

Most experts agree that some violence is related to the stress that modern families encounter. Men who batter often tend to bury their feelings of anxiety, fear, or frustration until they lose control and explode in anger. Often these men don't know how to manage anger, how to cope with pressure, or how to deal with the economic difficulties of life.

Many abusive persons have low self-esteem. They have never had good male role models, they feel personally incompetent, and they are inclined to assert their masculinity by being tough and dominant. Sometimes fueled by alcohol or triggered by intense frustration, they become violent and attack their own spouses or children.[25]

Even Christian men can fall into the same patterns, and some come to the false conclusion that the Bible gives them permission to be dictators in their families. But the Bible teaches that husbands are to love their wives "just as Christ also loved the church and gave Himself for it" (Ephesians 5:25). A man is to be a servant to his family while at the same time being its leader. A husband and a father is to be a provider for his family. He is to take care of their physical needs by working and earning an income to help meet those needs. Then he is to protect them, not only from physical harm but from spiritual harm as well.

His is not an easy job, especially in difficult economic times when jobs are scarce or when two incomes are needed just to survive. In tough times, disappointments are frequent, and it is easy to react in anger; but abuse is never appropriate. A clear understanding of the God-ordained roles and relationship of husband and wife is needed to help prevent this type of failure in the family.

The Great Marital Bail-Out

God's plan for marriage is that a husband and wife should remain committed to each other for life. In more than half of all marriages today, however, it doesn't work out that way. Often divorce is more common than marriage, and divorces today are almost instantaneous.

Prior to the divorce reforms of the 1970s, most divorces were based upon the grounds of "fault." Generally one of the spouses had to be guilty of some act of unfaithfulness or misbehavior, such as adultery. More recently this has given way to "no fault" divorces. These "convenience" divorces have both weakened the institution of marriage and undermined the lifelong commitment that God ordained for marriage. The result has been a soaring rise in divorce rates.

For the past decade half of all marriages end in divorce, but one recent study predicts that three-fifths of current first marriages will end in divorce if current trends persist.[26]

"Divorce is always a lose-lose situation that leaves scars for both partners."

According to other demographic predictions, 90 percent of all baby boomers will marry at least once. About half of these will get at least one divorce, one in five will get two divorces, and 5 percent will divorce three times or more. According to some observers, baby boomers think the institution of marriage is great, but often they don't care much for their partners. So they divorce freely.[27]

Divorce is always a lose-lose situation that leaves scars for both partners. People who divorce usually suffer many stressful emotions, including loneliness, anger, remorse, depression, guilt, low self-esteem, and fear of failure. In terms of emotional impact, divorce is second only to the death of a spouse, and in many cases the experience of divorce is even more traumatic. While the man generally comes out a little better than the woman, there are no winners in divorce.

Who Will Save the Children?

"If the well-being of its children is the proper measure of the health of a civilization, the United States is in grave danger."

With these words, the editors of *Fortune* magazine introduced a special series of articles devoted to America's kids in crisis. According to the magazine:

> Of the 65 million Americans under 18, fully 20 percent live in poverty, 22 percent live in single-parent homes, and almost 3 percent live with no parent at all. Violence among the young is so rampant that the American Academy of Pediatrics calls it a public health emergency. The loss of childhood innocence is a recent phenomenon, affecting all income levels and ethnic groups. Playground fights that used to end in bloody noses now end in death. Schools that once considered talking in class a capital offense are routinely frisking kids for weapons, questioning them about drugs. AIDS has turned youthful experimentation with sex into Russian roulette. A good public education, safe streets, and family dinners—with both mother and father present—seem like quaint memories of a far distant past. The bipartisan National Commission on Children wrote in . . . its 1991 report, that addressing the unmet needs of American youngsters "is a national imperative as compelling as an armed attack or a natural disaster."[28]

The Bible has a great deal to say about children. The psalmist tells us that children are a gift from the Lord (Psalm 127:3). From Proverbs, we understand that child-rearing is critical in determining the direction of each child's life (Proverbs 22:6). Early in the Old Testament, Moses stressed the importance of biblical precepts as a guide for parenting (Deuteronomy 6:7), while Paul, in the New Testament, assures us that discipline is an act of parental love (Ephesians 6:4).[29]

We are often reminded that Jesus loves children (see Mark 10:13–16 for example), so we have plenty of evidence that children are important and that God wants us to love and instruct our children in ways that are consistent with God's Word. But today, many children aren't even allowed to be kids. Instead of viewing childhood as an age of innocence, we have begun to think of children as competent: to make their own decisions, to take care of themselves after school (and sometimes when they face danger in school), and to deal with a steady television diet of overt violence, explicit sexuality, and crisis issues that most kids in the sixties and seventies knew nothing about.

While parents are at work, children are often home watching the R-rated movies on cable TV. Television has become our children's primary source of information about issues from culture to morality. It is hardly surprising that young children start making adult-like decisions far before they reach an age of maturity.

Teenage and pre-teen sex has become the norm and, predictably, there has been a steady decline in the median age for first sexual contact, pregnancy, venereal disease, and AIDS. Teenage girls in America get pregnant at the rate of one million every year, twice the rate of England which is number two on the list.[30]

But many kids don't have to watch a video or turn on a television set to see adult scenes of substance abuse, violence, or sexual immorality. They see it in their own homes, watching their own parents and sometimes experiencing their wrath. Every day about three children die of injuries inflicted by abusive parents, and untold numbers are beaten up by the very people they should be able to love and trust.

When home life gets too hard, a lot of kids run away. Early in life they learn about drugs, and often they experiment with a variety of harmful substances, including alcohol, in an effort to find the acceptance they could never get from their parents.

It is hardly any wonder that we read statistics like this: "Every 24 hours, almost 3,000 children see their parents get divorced; 1,629 children are put in adult jails; 3,288 children run away from home; 1,512 drop out of school; and 7,742 teenagers become sexually active!"[31] "In 1990, a record 407,000 minors were taken from their parents and placed in foster homes—up 66 percent from 1983. While some of these forced separations were to protect kids from physical or sexual abuse, the majority stemmed from parental neglect or the inability of mothers and fathers to provide basic food, clothing, or shelter."[32]

Beyond the incidence of violent or self-destructive behavior in the home, other less physical problems can have an effect on the healthy development of our kids. Sometimes, for example, parents are guilty of "hurrying" their children to grow up too fast. In some cases, four-year-olds learn about AIDS, preschoolers are told about abuse and violence, and young children become knowledgeable about sex, drugs, and crime long before they are capable of assimilating the information. By the time these kids reach their teenage years, they can appear to be sophisticated beyond their years, and as a result, parents fail to set appropriate limits or to provide needed guidance. Teenagers are left on their own, and everyone is surprised when disaster strikes!

All together, these conditions have created havoc for the American family. Children as young as five years old are developing ulcers in response to stress.[33] The rate of depression is increasing, especially in more affluent communities, and suicide among young people continues to be a major problem. The suicide rate for adolescents has tripled since 1973 and now ranks as the third leading cause of death among children.[34]

In sum, a lot of our children are paying the price for our lack of traditional family values and our failure to give guidance, direction, and models of morality and self-control.

The family is supposed to be a place of security and love, but for many children, it's the place of insecurity, anger, abuse, and terror.[35] In 1986 more than one million children nationwide experienced demonstrable harm as a result of maltreatment (neglect or physical, psychological, or sexual abuse), and 1,100 died as a result of abuse or neglect.

Most of the adults who abuse children were themselves abused as youngsters; and when abused children grow up, they frequently become spouse abusers, child abusers, and even abusers of their own elderly parents. Such violence completes a cycle that often goes on for generations. It is sad to realize that most of the people incarcerated for violent crimes have been victims of child abuse, and many have been arrested for violence against their own children or spouses.[36]

As we have seen, many children live with violence and fear throughout their lives.

The stories are no longer strange or shocking; they appear in our newspapers almost every day. They are evidence of the tragedy of life without God in the self-indulgent, self-seeking culture of the 1990s. Writer Ronald Henkoff is right when he says, "Kids are killing, dying, bleeding. America is in the midst of a raging epidemic of juvenile homicide, suicide, and abuse."[37]

What will it take for America to wake up to these disasters?

8

GOD'S DESIGN

A friend of mine, a psychologist, recently told me about a speech that was given by the retiring president of the American Psychological Association. Usually these speeches are technical discussions of research and other weighty professional issues, but Dr. Stanley R. Graham did something very different. He reflected on the history of his profession, talked a little about his own family and career, made some observations about the women's movement and the more recent men's movement, and then concluded with his perspective of "what a man wants" in life. I think the following excerpt from Dr. Graham's remarks makes fascinating reading. He said:

> I am ready to tell you, at least from my perspective, what a man wants. He wants his children to grow and mature to be wise and capable, independent and self-reliant, and yet he longs to hold them in the palm of his hand as he did on the day of their birth. He wants to be able to subdue his pride and forgive their brusqueness so he can remain close to them until they see his caring. He wants to be free to express his caring as David did when he cried, "Absalom, my son, my son, would that I had died for thee" (2 Samuel 18:33). Although father and son seem made for contention, they derive their highest sense of pride from one another. He wants to admire his daughter's beauty

161

and grace, for each girl child's beauty is unique in the eyes of her father. At the same time, he wants to honor her wit and intellect so that the complete human being that she becomes is not obscured by artificial sentimentality. He wants his mate's love and caring without having to ask for it, and he wants to be able to show his love for her without having to be concerned that it undermines his image of manhood. He hates to see himself as a tearful, weak creature, dependent on others for his sense of affirmation. But he is tired of hiding his tears and turning away to preserve some traditional image of manhood.[1]

This is a sensitive and thoughtful summary of what one man wants for his life, especially for his life as a family member. I would guess that most people have dreams about what they want for their lives and for their families, but how many of us stop to ask *what God wants?*

What Does God Want for Families?

God has a plan for family happiness and success. God Himself instituted marriage, and He gave us the only workable blueprint for successful family living. God's plan recognizes Christ as the head of the home. It is a plan that recognizes male and female roles and values the unique contributions of each.

It is a plan that respects both children and parents, that does not disdain the elderly, that honors work regardless of the worker's age or sex, that encourages the joy of marital intimacy, that forgives sin and failure, and that expresses concern for single people, including single parents.

God never promises that those who keep His plan will be spared from family problems; we all live in a sinful, stress-filled world. But He does promise to honor and to love those generations of families that seek to live in accordance with His guidelines (Psalm 103:17, 18).

Family counselor George Rekers has written that the expectations one has for a family depend upon whether the family is viewed as a human invention of convenience or as a divinely created institution. In our society, many believe that the family is a social convention involving human agreements based upon rights and convenience. Such a view offers no concept of accountability to God as Creator or as head of the home.

"In stark contrast to these self-centered beliefs, God's family plan is built on the relationship of men, women, and children to God."

Decisions regarding fidelity, commitment, whether or not to have children, or the discipline of those children are all viewed as personal choices. When problems occur in marriage, the decision to stay with one's mate or to abandon the relationship also is made as a matter of rights and personal choices. Often, secular families are molded around some notion of "fulfillment" or of gaining some sort of personal benefit or advantages from one's role in the family.

In stark contrast to these self-centered beliefs, God's family plan is built on the relationship of men, women, and children to God. While individual differences are respected and individual decisions are encouraged, family members are accountable to one another and to God.

Families are to live in accordance with biblical guidelines. From Scripture they know that the marriage union reflects the relationship of God to human beings and that the family unit reflects how God relates to His church. For the Christian, the central purpose of the family is to glorify God and to advance His kingdom. The home is not merely a "filling station" where various family members drop in to have their needs serviced. Instead, the home is to be a place where human beings live together with a commitment to fulfill God's plan and purpose.

How does this plan work in practice? To answer that question, I would like to look briefly at God's plan for marriage, for masculinity and femininity, for parent-child relationships, and for intimacy. All of these are discussed in the Bible, but they are not limited to one place or time in history. Biblical guidelines go beyond culture; that is one reason why Judeo-Christian ideals have survived for centuries and in so many societies.

I agree with pastor and author Gene Getz who wrote that it is "only as we evaluate ourselves in the light of biblical—not cultural—criteria that we can truly build a New Testament home," one that is consistent with God's plan for the family.

God's Plan for Marriage

If we take the Bible seriously, we have to conclude that marriage was instituted by God. It is not a relationship of mere human convenience.

The basic purpose of marriage is to provide "union" and "companionship." At the time of creation, God knew that it was not good for a man to be alone, so He created the woman to be a suitable companion. The two were to become close, like one flesh, meeting each other's need for love and companionship. They were to enjoy each other sexually and to bear children. The Christian view of marriage emphasizes the dignity and sanctity of the physical union of a man and wife that is approved by God Himself.

Because it is a sacred bond, marriage must never be entered thoughtlessly nor terminated lightly. It involves a promise of genuine commitment on the part of both husband and wife. Good marriages are built on love. But "love" has become a confusing word in our culture, so we need to realize that genuine love involves both feelings and thinking. Anybody who has been "in love" knows that emotions run high, that the world looks bright, and that lovers are filled with warm feelings and excitement. But this giddy kind of emotional high will not last. Relationships that are mostly emotional are hard to sustain when the passion fades. While the love in a healthy marriage never dies, the passion always fades.

Several years ago, University of Minnesota researchers studied love relationships and noted the relatively short life of "passionate love." "If the inevitable odds against eternal passionate love in a relationship were better understood, more people might choose to be satisfied with the quieter feelings of satisfaction and contentment," these researchers concluded. They went on to suggest that "the sharp rise in the divorce rate in the past two decades is linked, at least in part, to the growing importance of intense positive emotional experiences (romantic love) in people's lives, experiences that may be particularly difficult to sustain over time."[2]

Lasting love, therefore, also has a rational side. This concerns commitment, decision-making, and loving actions. But even as feeling without thinking can be lopsided, so can love that is all intellectual and duty-driven but with no emotion. When feelings are all gone, the marriage is vulnerable to breaking up, especially should someone else appear on the scene who appeals to the emotional side of one of the partners.

The kind of love on which healthy marriages are built is a love that is both emotional and rational. It is a love that is emotionally intense, at least at times, but also consistent, caring, sustaining, and built on an unwavering rational commitment of the husband and wife to each other.

As described in the Bible, this kind of love is kind, patient, and concerned about the well-being of others. People who love one another are people who learn to communicate with one another. They are willing to express their hopes and fears, their joys and disappointments, their successes and failures, not solely because they feel like doing this, but because they want to understand one another better. God, who is love, gives us the capability of loving our mates with an in-depth love, and of showing love, as well, to our family members, our neighbors, and even our enemies.

Becoming One

The words "one flesh" are found in Genesis 2:24, and quoted several times in the New Testament (Matthew 19:5; Mark 10:8; 1 Corinthians 6:16; Ephesians 5:31). In the context where these words are usually used, God presents Eve to Adam to be his companion, and Adam immediately recognizes that she is one of his kind. In other words, they are the same flesh. Jesus referred to this when He quoted Genesis 2:24 and reminded His listeners that the married are no longer two. They have been joined together (literally, "yoked") by God Himself.

This relationship involves a sexual, emotional, and spiritual bond between the husband and wife. There is no implication that the two should try to squelch their personalities; neither is one to dominate and overpower the other. Instead, married couples are intended to form a team that is to work together for the good of one another and the family.

According to the Bible, marriage involves an agreement between two equals, a man and a woman, who are willing to submit to one another. This is the ideal on which every Christian marriage should be based. The man and the woman submit themselves to one another under the authority of God (Ephesians 5:21). They determine to love and encourage each other and are devoted to doing whatever is necessary to support one another's spiritual, physical, and emotional needs. Each agrees to "forsake all others," giving each other the exclusive right to meet intimate needs.

> *"According to the Bible, marriage involves an agreement between two equals, a man and a woman, who are willing to submit to one another."*

This does not mean that the husband and wife are to withdraw from the world in an effort to spend life together on a perpetual honeymoon. We live and work and worship in groups, and we all function best in the company of other people. But the husband and wife have a unique commitment to each other. As they meet one another's needs within marriage, ideally they establish a pattern for meeting the needs of their children as well. And from there the family relates to others in the extended family and in the community.

When one or both partners in the marriage feels frustration because needs are not being met or because the relationship has grown tired or sour, there is greater vulnerability for affairs or for the marriage to deteriorate. In times like this we are tempted to assume, falsely, that some person other than one's spouse is better able to meet needs. For a time this might happen, but eventually the new relationship also grows flat and unfulfilling and the self-centered participants find that their actions have left behind a trail of broken, rejected people, including young children.

In our society, it is common to believe that two people are not likely to meet one another's needs for a lifetime. When a couple feels that they are no longer meeting each other's needs, they may choose to separate and to find new partners.

As a pastor, I have counseled hundreds, perhaps thousands of couples who were having difficulties in their marriages. I sometimes think I have heard every possible excuse for breaking the marriage commitment. While my heart goes out to those who struggle with their marriages, I can state with certainty that those who have violated God's plan for their marriages have always lived to reap the consequences of their decisions.

Pastors don't always have a good image in our contemporary society, but they are the people who do much, if not most, of the marriage counseling with hurting people. It is not an easy job. On the one hand, I am called to express the love and compassion of Christ. I know about the importance of listening in counseling, and I have heard person after person glibly tell me that going their own ways would all work out for the best. My heart aches when I think of those who have ignored God's love and plan for their marriages and have encountered a lot of unnecessary pain as a result.

On the other hand, as a pastor, I am called to teach and to maintain the standards of biblical living. The same counselors who listen must also express their care by informing people when they are violating God's commands and doing what is wrong. Telling people that they are wrong is never easy, even if this is done gently. But I have learned over the years that genuine love is not saying what people *want to hear*, but saying what they *need to hear*. More than ever before I am convinced that people need to hear and heed God's instructions for marriage and marital happiness. God wants us to have happy and fulfilling marriages. But this only will happen when we are willing to follow God's design for marriage.

Marriages That Last

Dr. Jim Conway spent thirty years as a pastor before earning two doctor's degrees and moving to the west coast where he and his wife, Sally, are involved in teaching, writing, and counseling in the area of marriage and the family. For almost forty years, the Conways have sought to live out God's marriage plan in their own home, and recently they surveyed 186 couples to discover what makes a good marriage work in others.

In a book that described their findings, the Conways wrote that nearly every couple "starts their marriage with high expectations but then runs into snags, which have caused almost half of recent marriages to break apart. In addition, many of the couples who haven't divorced are very unhappy." But despite the widespread unhappiness and the high divorce rate, couples with successful and happy marriages had determined to say "We don't care what the divorce statistics show or what anybody else is doing. We are going to make this marriage work!"[3]

These are not bull-headed couples who deny reality and pretend to be happy when they are miserable. They are couples who have applied godly principles to their own lives and marriages. And their marriages are good. According to Jim and Sally Conway, ten traits emerged from their study that are crucial for holding a marriage together. Every one of these principles is consistent with God's Word, the Bible.

First on the list is a commitment to stay married and to keep their marriages a high priority. Even the infamous Dr. Kinsey agreed. After studying six thousand marriages and three-thousand divorces, his research team concluded that "there may be nothing more important in a marriage than a determination that it shall persist. With such a determination, individuals force themselves to adjust and to accept situations which would seem sufficient grounds for a breakup, if continuation of the marriage were not the prime objective."[4]

This kind of commitment is a choice in which couples agree to stay together, to love and affirm one another, to grow and to help each other grow. Genuine commitment involves a mutual caring where each person is concerned about the other's fulfillment and well-being and where a couple works together on problems, even though this is often a long and difficult process. And when a mate wants out, marriages still can be saved and often are, when one-half of the couple maintains commitment.

The second trait of a successful marriage is effective, mutually satisfying communication. All the marriage counseling books put this near the top of the list. When communication breaks down, so do marriages. When marriages begin to fail, so does communication.

Everybody knows that communication is not easy. It involves listening without being judgmental and jumping to conclusions, trying to understand one another, showing respect, disclosing what we really feel, and avoiding one-upmanship and put-down comments.

Communication takes time, effort, and sometimes a recognition that men and women tend to be different in their communication patterns. Women tend to share themselves—

their dreams, their problems, their joys, their feelings. Men, in contrast, tend to be more focused on solving problems, giving advice, and making plans. Sometimes men dismiss what their wives say as small talk; women are annoyed that men aren't more caring. Both can be afraid of rejection or of being hurt. In times of stress there is often silence or the opposite, shouting criticism and advice to one another. None of this contributes to healthy marriage.

> *"When husbands and wives take time to pray with one another and to bare their souls before God, they are building bridges of spiritual communication that could not be constructed in any other way."*

Third on the list is spiritual vitality. Several national surveys show that healthy marriages tend to build around commonly held religious values. Undoubtedly it is true that families and couples who pray together stay together.

Restoring the Family Through Prayer

When husbands and wives take time to pray with one another and to bare their souls before God, they are building bridges of spiritual communication that could not be constructed in any other way. When a husband is willing to pray with his wife, they both feel a greater sense of security in knowing that together they are open to finding the help and direction of God in their lives. When men and women are willing to pray, they really are saying; "We don't have all the answers, but we know who does!"

I can recall a number of times when I have counseled with married couples who are in crisis and seem to have reached an impasse in their marriages. But when we would finish talking, I would ask them to pray with me out loud. Often, as they would pray and acknowledge the real presence of God in their lives, they would be reminded that they were not alone in facing their problems. The prayer would alert them to the fact that God really was there in the midst of the crisis as together we called on Him and sought His help.

Effective conflict resolution is number four on the Conways' list. Consider this from a man who wrote a whole book about family fights:

> Whenever two or more people have a continuing relationship, there will eventually be conflict. Are you married? There will be conflict. Are you single and living at home with your parents? There will be conflict. Are you the parent of a single son or daughter living at home? There will be conflict. . . . And whenever there is conflict, there can only be one of two outcomes: We will either hurt—even destroy—each other, or we will build up each other and benefit from the experience.[5]

Couples with stable marriages learn how to solve differences and to benefit from the experience.

Energy from friends is the fifth trait that was identified. Friends sometimes create problems and put us under pressure, but without friends to encourage, love, talk to, worship with, and enjoy, our marriages are more likely to have problems. The Conways state this emphatically: "It doesn't matter whether your marriage is: new or seasoned; deliriously happy, comfortably content, boring, or coming apart; childless or child-full; rich, poor or in between; God-centered, church-centered or some other-centered; a first marriage for both or any combination of remarriage and blending. No matter what it's like, genuine friends are vital to the success of your marriage." The God who put us in families also put our marriages and families in communities where we need one another.

Number six is sexual intimacy. I once heard about a professor who went into a classroom and read an explicit description of sexual love-making. Then he asked the students to guess where he found the excerpt, and they all guessed wrong. The professor was reading from the Bible, from the Song of Solomon.

God, who made us sexual creatures, is not intent on killing the joy of sex. But He gave guidelines for the best possible sex, and that is within marriage. Couples who have good sexual relationships tend to have good marriages. Maybe it's impossible to say if one causes the other. But we do know that God's plan for marital fulfillment involves enjoyable sex.

The seventh trait of lasting marriages, time to laugh and play, doesn't appear often in books about marriage. Even God took time off after creating the world, and He expects us to take breaks as well.

This is not easy in a society where people work hard to make ends meet, to raise kids, to build careers, to pay the bills, and to handle their households. Busy people who fail to take time off to relax and to laugh tend to be up-tight people whose tension comes out in their marriages. We live in a society that prizes work, admires workaholics, and looks down on people who spend too much time "goofing off." A lot of companies and professions, including the ministry, are stocked with people who feel guilty when they take time away from work.

When marriages begin, the couple usually takes time to be with one another and often they have fun together. When they get busy with their lives and fail to enjoy one another, they not only violate God's plan for marriage; they put tremendous pressure on their relationship.

Developing Realistic Expectations

Couples that have lasting marriages also learn to develop realistic expectations. This is trait number eight.

In the early years, couples sometimes enter marriage with the idea that they will transform a mate and mold one's spouse into the near-perfect creature that they have always wanted. Forget it! Of course we all change in marriage. Hopefully this is because we are all growing. But in healthy marriages, we learn to accept the fact that some things will never change. We become more realistic and learn to live with and sometimes even grow to appreciate the differences.

The ninth trait, serving one another, gets us to one of the most misunderstood and controversial elements in God's marriage plan: the idea of submission.

It is true that millions of men have abused, mistreated, and battered women into submission and fear. Most family violence and abuse comes from men. Some even comes from men who claim to be Christians and who use Ephesians 5:22 ("Wives, submit to your own husbands, as to the Lord") as a hammer to pound their wives into submission. Too often that extends to families where the father self-righteously demands that he be obeyed without question because he is the head of the home. He acts like a despot who demands compliance and cares little that he is disliked by everybody. I can think of one man who was so harsh and unloving, that he drove all five of his children into rebellion and lost them all.

Before the Bible says anything about wives submitting to their husbands, however, it commands both the husband and wife to submit to one another. Husbands are to commit themselves to the spiritual well-being of their wives and children. Wives are to commit themselves to the spiritual well-being of their husbands and their children. If both parties are committed to the best interests of the other, there would be minimal conflict in marriage. Sadly, selfish husbands often hurt their wives, and selfish wives often hurt their husbands. Selfishness destroys relationships.

While the Bible commands wives to "submit to your own husbands" (Ephesians 5:22), it does so in the context of commanding husbands to "love your wives" (Ephesians 5:25), like Christ loved the church. This is a giving, caring type of love that in no way implies male dominance. It is not one person as "the boss (generally the husband) and the other as a servant (often the wife). Instead, two servants offer to the other their gifts and abilities, each honoring, respecting and loving the other." Mutual submission implies cooperation.

Servant husbands and wives affirm one another, recognize the equality of the sexes, meet each other's needs, show mutual respect, and seek to encourage each other's unique gifts.

Item ten on the Conways' list, have a relationship that is alive and growing, may seem surprising, but I think that it, too, is biblical. Some people's whole lives have a couch-potato existence. They never try anything new, never do anything to stimulate their minds, never give any thought to spiritual growth, don't bother to keep in shape, and don't do much to expand their social contacts. Their lives become routine and dull and that, of course, extends to their marriages.

A lot of life is routine. It is not easy to avoid boring tasks, mundane duties, and dull jobs. But when we let our marriages slip into this kind of dullness, we set ourselves up for marital trouble and the possibility of breakup increases. Marriages grow stale when individuals and couples don't grow.

Jim and Sally Conway add a caution in their book that all of us should heed. The more we think about God's plan for our lives and our marriages, the easier it is to think that we can't make it. But the God who gives us a blueprint for living, also gives us strength for the journey. God's standards are high; our goal is to do the best we can, in His strength, to live increasingly according to the divine plan. Jesus said, "without Me you can do nothing" (John 15:5), but when He is in our lives we can say with the Apostle Paul, "I can do all things through Christ who strengthens me" (Philippians 4:13).

God's Plan for Men in Families

Something has happened to men in the past few years. For almost a generation we males have watched women define their roles, deal with their insecurities, clarify what it means to be female, and think about their place in society. Sometimes we do not like what the feminist movement says, especially when we see radical feminists seeking to destroy the family. But we agree that many women are abused and treated unfairly, and that is not right. Most of us believe that women should have greater access to better jobs and that they shouldn't have to face "invisible ceilings" in so many work places. Women do have concerns that need to be addressed and inequities that need to be corrected.

Where does all of this leave men? As one leader in the new men's movement has written, we men have begun to realize that women are not the only gender with problems of identity. We men have problems too. We don't know what it means to be a man in this society. We are discovering that our macho-masculinity is harmful to people of both sexes. At last we are waking up to the fact that men have a lot of problems. We struggle with insecurities, relationships, finances, sex, careers, finding integrity as leaders, or dealing with temptations that come from our lusts, our desires to wield power, our love of money, and our temptations to be perfect. It has taken a while, but more and more men are also beginning to ask questions about spirituality and about what it means to be on earth, in the midst of the supersonic changes that are whizzing around us.

The Bible is not a question-answer book that lists all our problems and gives cookbook answers. It does give guidelines for living, however, and it does give us a model, Jesus Christ. We men have the challenge of following His example, as best we can and with divine help.

According to God's plan, men in families have at least two major responsibilities. They are to lead and they are to be loving.

Men Who Lead

Husbands and fathers play a key role in God's plan for the family. Men are to be spiritual leaders in their families.

The man is to understand his wife and children, meet their needs, encourage them through life's difficulties, motivate them, and teach his family the truths about God (Deuteronomy 6:4–9). Men must protect their families, provide for them, and give them a spiritual heritage that they can pass on to future generations. Even though no human being is perfect, the male leader is to seek to live like Christ and to be a model and mentor for his family.

The husband is to work at building a permanent relationship with his wife, one in which there is a sacrificial type of giving. As the spiritual leader in the home, the man must seek to help both his wife and his children to grow spiritually. The divine authority that a man has to be a spiritual leader is based on the authority that Christ has to lead the church. A well-balanced father does more than just "bring home the bacon." He is a leader and teacher who motivates his children to effective decision making. He is not afraid to correct them when they are wrong, but neither is he harsh, unreasonable, or demanding behavior of them that he himself is not willing to give. The balanced father loves his children enough to provide what they need. He listens to them, is sensitive to them, and helps them with their special problems and projects. He is one who is in fellowship with God and shares that fellowship with his children. Family leadership such as this is an awesome task; and as we have seen, when men disappear or abdicate their leadership responsibilities, the fallout in hurt lives is catastrophic.

I am convinced that too many men have failed to be leaders. They have failed to correct their children, to be present when needed, to be helpful and available to their lives, to provide spiritual leadership in the home. Part of our family and national problems come because men have failed as leaders.

Men Who Love

Leaders can be insensitive dictators, or they can be benevolent pacesetters who know how to take a firm stand even as they show sensitivity and care for those they lead. God's plan for men and for the family gives no place for the tough-as-nails, dictator type of male who does what he does with an iron hand. At times, men are to be tough, even as Christ was tough, but they are also to be tender and loving. They are told that their own spiritual lives will be hindered if they do anything less than treat their wives with consideration and respect (1 Peter 3:7).

The husband is to love his wife in the same compassionate, sensitive, consistent, self-sacrificing way that Christ loved the church and gave Himself for the church (Ephesians 5:23). And when the man raises his children, he is to bring them up in such loving discipline that even God Himself would approve.

Once again we see that God's standards are high. We can try hard to be loving leaders in our homes and to some extent we will be successful. But the real man of the house needs the help and guidance of the Holy Spirit as he fulfills his role.

God's Plan for Women in Families

Walk into any bookstore and you will find shelves of books about women, about their struggles, their femininity, their place in the society, their accomplishments, their emotions. Many of these books, some even written by men, discuss the place of women in society, in the work place, in the church, and at home.

Sometimes these books devalue women and present the idea that a woman's value is judged solely by her degree of commitment to four cardinal virtues: piety, purity, submissiveness, and domesticity. I certainly don't believe they are the only attributes of a Godly woman. However, I agree wholeheartedly that these four virtues properly defined are critical elements. Many times they are perceived as being characteristic of weakness. Nothing could be further from the truth. These blessed traits help compose the epitome of strength and discipline. They are not demeaning, nor are they constrictive. To the contrary, they are part of the fundamental makeup of a successful family.

When we think about God's plan for women in marriage and family relationships, two things are certain. First, there is a lot of misunderstanding and disagreement about the roles of women, and second, everybody agrees that women are not second class or second best.

Men and women were both created by God. They are of equal value, equally inclined to sin, and of equal importance. They both have a significant role to play in the home, and they both make significant contributions to the society.

Consider the virtuous woman who is described in Proverbs 31:10–31. This praiseworthy woman is intelligent, industrious, sincere, competent, and attractively dressed. She is described as being more valuable than rubies and one who is entirely trustworthy in every regard. She is depicted as an effective business woman who works in the community, but she also is committed to her family and actively involved in domestic duties. She can lead her children and follow her husband in such a way that she is a credit to both. She speaks with wisdom and kindness and does much to create the spiritual atmosphere of the home. Her children are highly complimentary, and her husband praises her because of her qualities, including the way she honors God and cares for her family.

This doesn't sound like Roseanne or the angry descriptions that come from radical feminists, but neither does it sound like those descriptions of women as dowdy housewives with dull, inactive minds.

God sees women as valuable human beings, made in the divine image. Like men who never marry, some women stay single and make a contribution without the companionship of a mate. The majority, however, become wives and mothers. All three roles—person, wife, mother—are important.

Consider, first, the woman as a person. The Bible gives many examples of capable women who played significant roles in their societies, not because they were women or in spite of the fact that they were women, but because they were competent, committed to God, and available to make a difference. The "true womanhood" traits of piety, purity, submissiveness, and domesticity are admirable and worth developing, but they are not the only traits of God-pleasing women. Many women are creative, sensitive, and competent in their fields of interest, with special abilities in the areas of leadership, organization, and hospitality. These, too, are admirable female traits.

"Children learn their basic concepts of security, interdependence and respect for authority from observing the relationship of a wife and husband."

In addressing the church, in Romans 12, the Apostle Paul described the spiritual gifts that are given to followers of Jesus Christ. Some people are especially gifted to teach, serve, encourage others, give, lead, or show mercy, for example. But there is nothing to suggest that these special capabilities come to men only.

The true woman seeks to develop her fullest potential. If she is married, this growth should come with the support and encouragement of her husband. Read the history of first-century Israel, and you will discover that Christians were active in promoting the liberation of women centuries before the feminist movement ever appeared.

The wife in God's plan is to love and to respect her husband, even as she works in partnership alongside him. Some women may bristle at the biblical statement that they are the "weaker" half of the marriage partnership, but Bible scholars agree that this refers to physical strength and has nothing to do with moral stamina, strength of character, or mental capacity. In many homes, these characteristics are seen most clearly in the wives, especially if their husbands are gone or have failed in their responsibilities to be loving leaders in their homes.

I once heard about a cartoon where a husband and his several kids were trying to survive while the mother of the family was away temporarily. One of the kids was on the phone telling a friend that she was there with her father, her brothers, and her sisters, and even the family dog, but that "Mommy has left us all alone."

Most of us can relate to the little girl. Even in families where the husband pitches in and works hard to help with domestic and child-rearing responsibilities, it seems that the mother's presence and contribution is essential. Her attitude toward her husband and her children has a significant impact on the tone of the household and on how children view their families. This, in turn, translates into attitudes that last well into adulthood.

Children learn their basic concepts of security, interdependence, and respect for authority from observing the relationship of a wife and husband. They need to observe a dad who leads the family with love and treats his wife with respect, but they also need to observe a mother who appreciates and accepts her husband's role in the family and treats him with respect.

It is no secret that the challenges and responsibilities of motherhood have changed radically during the past several decades. Today a mother often must be an efficiency expert, economist, bargain hunter, affectionate lover, child guidance counselor, communications expert, and, as the kids get older, an on-call chauffeur. If the mother also works outside the home, she has the added challenge of juggling schedules and keeping both her family and her employer happy. Mothers deserve a lot more credit than they get for their sacrifices and significant roles they play in working to make their families function effectively.

God's Plan for Parent-Child Relationships

Following the political conventions that launched the 1992 presidential election campaigns, an artist for the *Cincinnati Enquirer* drew a cartoon with three panels. One panel was a drawing of the Congress building. The second was a picture of the White House. The third showed a parent, sitting in a rocking chair reading to a little kid. Underneath these drawings there were eight words: "Choose the real seat of power in America."

Children are a gift from God. Sometimes couples experience the pain of infertility and long for the gift that they have not been able to bear. In other cases, the gift comes before it was expected, or parents feel overwhelmed because they have more of these gifts than they feel equipped to handle.

Handling kids has never been easy, but today perhaps it is more difficult than ever. Unlike previous eras when the parents had the greatest influence on children for several years, we now live in a time when television and other influences come into the home early and start having a significant impact, even before children go to nursery school. The intensified pulls and pressures of our fast-paced society grab for parental attention and interfere with the compassionate caring, patient teaching, and loving discipline that children need, now more than ever.

Despite influences that make parenting difficult, we need to remember that God chose to put innocent and helpless human beings into the care of young, often inexperienced men and women who live in families. These parents have one major mission: to teach their children to be independent and God-respecting adults, who will take their places of responsibility in society and in turn will contribute to rearing the next generation. This challenge involves two overlapping duties: teaching children and disciplining them.

Teaching Children

Everybody knows that teaching involves more than giving instruction. In the Old Testament, when God was beginning to reveal His plan for parenting, He told the early believers to be sure that their own lives were in order spiritually. Then they were to teach their children diligently, by words and by example, whenever the opportunity arose, night or day (Deuteronomy 6:5–7). The teaching surely involved the practicalities of how to live, but it also involved the teaching of values, attitudes, and spiritual truths. Surely these early people taught the Ten Commandments and, as Ted Koppel is reported to have said in a commencement address, these were never presented as the Ten Suggestions.

Parents today cannot expect the secular society to train their children in biblical knowledge or in spiritual values. This is a role that belongs to parents. It takes time and energy, words and modeling. The old adage is true that often actions speak louder than words. Our children and our families will never learn stable values only in school, and neither will they reach spiritual maturity solely by attending church or religious functions. This teaching must go beyond school classrooms or Sunday mornings so that children see time-tested values in the lives of their parents. Like Joshua in the Old Testament, family leaders today, especially fathers, need to say "But as for me and my house, we will serve the Lord"

(Joshua 24:15). This must be supplemented by parental behavior that is authentic and consistent, not hypocritical.

As teachers of their children, parents should do what they
can to give their kids the attention that they need. This is
very difficult for many of us, but nothing hurts a parent-child
relationship like neglect. Such neglect may begin unnoticed,
but in time it will take its toll on the life of the whole family.

> *"Parents today cannot expect the
> secular society to train their
> children in biblical knowledge or in
> spiritual values. This is a role that
> belongs to parents."*

I can think of a family where the children were allowed to
run wild. In an effort to let the kids "develop their own
lifestyles and decide for themselves what to believe," the parents let their children do anything they pleased. By their
teenage years, these young people were involved in drinking,
sex, and eventually drugs. Both kids dropped out of school.
The girl got pregnant and had an abortion. The son became
a drug pusher in one of our major cities.

By the time the parents began asking what was going
wrong, it was already too late. Billy Sunday, the great evan-
gelist from the previous century, is said to have wept in his
old age because he had won the masses to Christ, but lost his
own children! Yet sadly, we need not go back to a past century to find other examples.

As we have seen in earlier chapters, our children are
bombarded on all sides by messages that encourage them to

do what is right in their own eyes. This blitz of information and secular values leaves them vulnerable to confusion and temptation. Parents, therefore, need to teach the moral values and the family values that are being criticized, often by media people and sometimes even by politicians in the current political climate.

Child Discipline

Discipline is not a popular word. It implies restraint, including self-restraint, and that goes against our natural inclinations to do what we feel like doing. But we all know that restraint is necessary sometimes. That is why we have prisons. That is why we tell a four year old that he cannot play in the busy street even though he feels like doing so.

Effective discipline begins with the parent, not the child. Parents must be willing to discipline themselves in order to love, instruct, and discipline their children consistently. Discipline and love go together, and parents are not to be so demanding, insensitive, and unloving that they discourage or embitter their children and provoke them to rebellion. Instead, we need balance. Parents must learn to say "I love you" and must demonstrate this consistently, but at the same time they must let children know that because of this love, there are certain things that, for their own good, children cannot be allowed to do.

The goal of discipline is not to punish or to gain dictatorial control. Discipline exists to correct the attitudes and actions of young people and to train them in the way that they should go.

One of the great promises of the Bible is found in Proverbs 22:6, "Train up a child in the way he should go, and when he is old, he will not depart from it." Bible scholars don't always agree about the exact meaning of these words. Some feel it means that if the right kind of training is provided, then the parental training should automatically be successful.

Others view this as a statement encouraging parents to develop the natural abilities of the child. I believe that these words from the Bible represent one of God's great promises to us as parents. The force of the original language implies that

---

"A parent may never be able to eliminate all of the damage that was done in the past, but there is always hope for the future. Even the prodigal son turned around and so have millions of young people since."

---

as the child grows older, he or she will not depart from the foundational training that was given in the beginning. Some have noted that the word "train" in the Hebrew means to train the palate or the mouth.

The imagery is taken from that of a Hebrew mother training her baby to begin eating solid food. I am convinced that as children develop an "early taste" for certain behaviors, values, and attitudes, these tend to stay with them throughout life. This gives parents a powerful directive to teach clearly, sometimes using loving discipline.

Perhaps every parent feels that he or she has failed, at least partially, in this training process. But there is hope. God is forgiving, and often He turns our failures around. A parent may never be able to eliminate all of the damage that was done in the past, but there is always hope for the future. Even the prodigal son turned around and so have millions of young people since.

The biblical account of the life of Jacob is an encouraging example of this. Almost everything that could go wrong in one man's life went wrong in his. He had children by several different women. There was division, envy, and hatred throughout his family. His jealous children were in constant competition for leadership in the family. The only godly child that he had was rejected by the others and eventually sold into slavery. Repeatedly, Jacob made the wrong choices and suffered the consequences. But there came a time in his life, when he finally took responsibility for his own actions. He acknowledged his sin and failure and cried out to God who heard him. Eventually his lost son was returned to him, his children turned around, and the family was reunited. God still hears prayers about our families, and He still forgives, even though the results in your family may be different than the events that happened in the family of Jacob. God's ways have not changed.

Parenting Goes Two Ways

An arresting cover on *Newsweek* magazine showed two women, one elderly, the other middle aged. Under the title of the cover story the magazine printed these words: "The Average American Woman Spends 17 Years Raising Children and 18 Years Helping Aging Parents." Inside, readers were introduced to Dot von Gerbig. When she was widowed in 1969, her parents moved in to help, but now, more than twenty years later, the parents are both legally blind. The mother is 84 and mentally confused. The father is 92 and confined to a wheelchair. They are completely dependent on their daughter, now in her early fifties, who works full time.

Assisted by her second husband and her fifteen-year-old son, von Gerbig is one of the estimated two million, middle aged American women who feels the economic and emotional stress of trying to nurture two generations at the same time.

The numbers of adult children who care for their elderly parents is likely to increase as our over-sixty-five generation gets progressively larger. Elder abuse is becoming a major problem. People across the country were horrified recently when newspapers nationwide reported that an old man had been abandoned by his daughter at a race track. When police traced the man's identity and found his daughter, several hundred miles away, they learned that the woman had become so overwhelmed by the needs of her aging parent that she tried to abandon him.

God's plan for grown children and grandchildren is that they should care for their older relatives, but at times these care-givers will need help. Some help might come from the government, but much must come from the churches. This kind of elder-care is a part of family living, and it expresses the kind of religion that pleases God Himself (1 Timothy 5:1–8; James 1:27).

Solo Parenting

In our discussions of parenting, we must not forget that millions of families in this country are headed by parents without partners. These are people who struggle with the challenges of raising children without the presence or encouragement of a mate, and often without additional financial support.

Sometimes these solo parents have contributed to bringing on their own problems, but often they are widows or victims of a divorce that they never wanted and even tried to prevent. Many feel guilty, angry, and inadequate. Perhaps most feel burned out at times, and overwhelmed by the family and financial stresses that they have to encounter alone.

Regardless of the circumstances that have led to their single state, parents without partners deserve the support, love, help, and encouragement of people in their communities and churches. Too often they don't get it. Instead they feel the disapproval and distrust that comes from insensitive people who should know better. God's plan for the family certainly extends to single-parent families who need His help and the help of others as they seek to raise their children without the presence of a partner.

God's Plan for Sexuality

We live in a sex-saturated society. The evidence of this is all around—in the media, the schools, the entertainment and advertising industries; even in government, business, and the military. We don't talk much about sex in the churches, but we read a lot about it in the Bible. And we discover there that God's plan for human sexuality is a lot different than the sexually-explicit values that permeate our culture.

Sex was created by God. It was His idea. But we humans were not created to be the same as animals, with uncontrolled appetites to be satisfied at will. We were given the ability to think, to recognize the consequences of our actions, to be compassionate, to have understanding, and to plan. We were given minds and we were given sexual bodies, with hormones and with the ability to enjoy sexual ecstasy. Adam and Eve were not ashamed of their nakedness, and they were very willing to comply when God told them to engage in the sexual action that would enable them to be fruitful and to multiply.

Like the manufacturer who gives instructions with his products, God gave us directions about how sex could ultimately be most fulfilling. The answer was that sexual intercourse should be within marriage. That, of course, is a view that is laughed at by our society, but it is a viewpoint that has led to massive and widespread misery.

Even Magic Johnson—who does not advocate that sex should be limited to marriage—agrees that promiscuity can lead to a host of problems. In a nationally-televised press conference, he said:

> I know all too well that having sex too early sets a pattern for your life that's hard to break. I found myself having sex with one person after another, and I put myself and my partner at more and more risk of getting HIV or another STD or getting pregnant. . . . If I had known what I do now when I was younger, I would have postponed sex as long as I could.

Too bad it took a tragedy in his life to bring this point home. God's plan is that sex be postponed until marriage. It always has been.

There are reasons for this. Sex apart from marriage can lead to the kinds of problems that Magic Johnson spoke about, and more. God wants to spare us from the pain of broken relationships, unwanted pregnancies, distrust, blows to self-esteem, sexual addictions, physical and sexual violence, and other types of sexually-produced miseries. And God wants us to avoid immoral behavior because it lowers sex to a physical relationship and fails to recognize that sex is really an emotional, physical, and spiritual experience.

Married sexual love is exclusive. Sex is to be preserved for the one person who makes a vow before God to stay with you for a lifetime. Certainly God did not blush when He inspired the poet of the Song of Songs to vividly portray the ecstasy of sex in marriage. God commands His married children to make love. He designed them to fit together for more than procreation. Their union brings together the three circles of love—unselfish giving, personal sharing, and pleasure-filled physical union—into a holy picture of the oneness of the Trinity and Christ's intimacy with the church. The depth of this sexual experience exceeds the shallow temporary thrills of Satan's counterfeit affairs.

Because sex is sacred, the devil wants to destroy it. He wants to convince us that sex limited to marriage is an old-fashioned and prudish idea, that God doesn't really care what we do with our bodies, and that healthy hormones deserve to be gratified. He doesn't even mind if we laugh, flippantly, and say "the devil made me do it." Along with a multitude of voices in the society that he dominates, the evil one even convinces us that we have no choice, that abstinence is asinine and pretty much impossible.

But self-control is possible, with God's help, and impurity is condemned so strongly and so often in the Bible, that it must be as devastating as the world around us is beginning to discover.

The Secret of Forgiveness

There is one important postscript in this picture of healthy sexuality. It centers around the word *forgiveness*. God who has high standards, forgives us when we fail. Maybe there is no better example anywhere than the well-known relationship of David and Bathsheba. Following their adultery and subsequent pregnancy, David tried to cover his sin, even to the point of having Bathsheba's husband killed. David felt guilty and ashamed of his action until he confessed his sin and found God's forgiveness.

Doesn't this give modern people license to do what they please sexually since they know that God will always forgive? David's life shows that the answer is a firm no. He was forgiven, but his reputation was tainted forever. The child that Bathsheba bore died and remained dead forever, like Urriah, Bathsheba's husband. And life for King David was never quite the same again.

When we ignore, rebel against, or fail to follow God's plan for our lives and marriages, there will be the opportunity for forgiveness and restoration—at least until God chooses to withdraw this offer. But the consequences of casting aside God's plan for the family are also likely to exist. As we have seen in earlier pages, those consequences are tearing families apart and ripping at the fabric of our country.

Can anything be done, now, before it is too late?

The answer is yes. We need to pull together, millions of us, to create the new American family.

9

THE NEW AMERICAN FAMILY

W e hear a lot about "family values" today. Slogans are used and statistics are quoted to support one agenda or another, and for nearly forty years now, the traditional family has been under intense pressure. Subtle messages from the secular culture tell us that marriage and child-rearing are little more than temporary arrangements. Commitment and sacrifice are out, and self-gratification is in; and the idea of "diversity" is a pretext for legitimizing lifestyles and behaviors recognized as immoral throughout recorded history.

But despite all the rhetoric and debate, the family unit endures much the same as it always has. And though families have been abused, misused, distorted, and frequently broken, the definitive nature of the family remains unchanged. We must not forget that the family was designed by God, and its constitution is unchangeable. No matter how troubled it

195

sometimes appears, the family is sacred to God, and its importance in society is not subject to whim.

Times change; values do not. The values upon which families have been built through countless generations are the same values upon which we build our families today. And no matter what difficulties we may encounter in the process, there is hope for the family in America, and there is hope for your family.

This hope lies in our resolve to abide by God's standards. If we recognize the importance of the family as the foundational institution of society—the first created by God—and if we are committed to the importance of building families on the time-tested principles of our faith, then there can be renewal and prosperity in homes all across this land. Make no mistake about it: preserving our families will take time and hard work. The family must become a personal priority, not one relegated to weekend hours. Our children cannot be parented merely "after five." Maintaining our families in this fast paced world will require changing our schedules, our priorities, our lifestyles. If we are to save the families of America— if *you* are to preserve your own family—then we must be willing to invest ourselves.

As individuals, churches, and communities, we must work to help restore the role of the family as the cornerstone of a free society. While we need to emphasize the importance of permanence and commitment in marriage, we also need to embrace those who are struggling. Men and women whose lives are fragmented—those who are coping with the trauma of loss and separation so common in these troubled times—need our love and support. Even as we hold up the standard of fidelity and perseverance, we cannot fail to aid those who have been wounded by this generation of social disorientation.

Addressing the Critical Issues

Let's examine certain issues in more detail: the structure and status of the family, the claims being made upon it by various agents promoting change, and the genuine sources of empowerment. The foundational principles of the family have long been established by history, theology, and tradition. But because of the vast number of attacks being made upon the

---

"I adamantly resist any "family agenda" set by government, based on principles which do not acknowledge the centrality of faith and morality in the home."

---

institution of the family by forces of every description, I want to clarify and reaffirm these principles. I want to challenge you to renew your commitment to fight for the American family, and I want to offer some proven strategies for bringing about change.

I certainly agree with the political figures who are saying that government policy should be "pro-family." But I adamantly resist any "family agenda" set by government, based on principles which do not acknowledge the centrality of faith and morality in the home. I am convinced that the kind of government support we need will not come from the liberal special interest groups or from congressional lobbies. It will only come when men and women at the grass roots make the "family" their top priority and when we each transform our convictions into power at the polls and through persistent political action.

Those who share these views must elect—and hold accountable—men and women committed to enacting legislation and programs that will help to restore the authority and autonomy of the traditional family. If the family should, indeed, fail, or if perverse activists and public officials legislate away its legitimate rights and privileges, we will be the ones to blame. And you and I will be accountable before God.

Let's be realistic. The family is not some ideal or imaginary institution but real people with very real problems. This raises a very interesting paradox: the family is our greatest source of strength, but it also demands the most effort and commitment from us.

There are times of tremendous happiness and satisfaction in the family, but there are other times when family problems create incredible stress. This is natural, of course, but the constant tension between these two extremes means that we must try to reduce the stress and increase the joy in the family. This can only happen if the family becomes a priority in our lives. We must apply our focused creativity and our best efforts toward ensuring that the family remains the nurturing, life-giving source it was designed to be.

Motives and Ambitions

As I have tried to show throughout this book, a vast difference of opinion exists about how to restore the fortunes of the American family. Some of those who give the most vehement speeches in favor of "family values" actually distort information and statistics to serve their own ends. Others attempt to define "family" in such broad terms that the word is virtually meaningless.

One member of Congress recently claimed, for example, that "traditional families" are on the edge of extinction and that just 7.1 percent of American families are still traditional. That number was shockingly low. But when asked to explain his definition of the term "traditional family," the politician said he was referring to homes where "there is a husband working outside the home and a wife who is a homemaker with two children, both of whom are at home." Even if that might have been a satisfactory definition fifty years ago, it would be unrealistic to apply such a restrictive standard today. By this definition, I wouldn't have a traditional family because I have three grown children, all married, not living at home. Not many of us would fit that model.

This is the danger of a politically correct definition designed by special interest groups. These liberal activists have no interest in supporting the traditional family—they are out to redefine the family and, by implication, to destroy it. If they could show that the traditional family is dead or dying, and that society is in need of a new statistical model, then they are in a much better position to introduce a definition of their own design which better suits their hidden agenda for radical social reform and political control.

These people play on public ignorance, disinterest, and political naiveté. It is to their advantage to justify their claim, for example, that a family with a wife working outside the home is "non-traditional." It is even to their advantage to show that a young couple, a husband and wife married and committed to each other for life but with only one child, is non-traditional. Why? Because their goal is to say, "The traditional family no longer exists, and there is nothing to replace it." If such an assertion were accepted, then whatever they chose to call family would become the model in designing a new, radical, social agenda.

The Nuclear Family

Throughout the history of the United States, the traditional Judeo-Christian family—often called the nuclear family—has been the accepted model for family life. Like the model of the atom, with a group of related components in orbit together within a finite "nucleus" of space, the family is defined both by its internal relationships and its external boundaries. It has nothing to do with atomic energy, of course, but with the predictable form and orderly relationships within the family. This unity of design and purpose gives the nuclear family its name.

Americans have always defined the family as that institution whose members are related by birth, heterosexual marriage, adoption, or legal custody. Changes come with age and maturity, with growth and loss, but that does not alter the basic definition. Whether or not the broad range of relationships in the traditional family can be described statistically is of far less importance than the recognition that the bond of relationships understood intuitively as "a family" is, in fact, the only definition of the family that counts. No manufactured, sexually deviant, or politically correct definition can ever replace that basic truth.

We believe that a family begins when a man and a woman are united in marriage—once commonly referred to as holy matrimony. The foundation of the family is the husband and wife, united in an emotional and physical relationship dedicated to their mutual benefit and founded on love. Statisticians may report that the average family has two, three, or more children, but any definition of the family must begin with the legal union of one man and one woman and a pledge of commitment.

From that point, there can be many modifications of the basic family unit. Some families have no children; some will have one or more children living at home; in others, the

---

"The foundation of the family is the husband and wife, united in an emotional and physical relationship dedicated to their mutual benefit and founded on love."

---

children may have already grown up and left home. Traditional families also include those homes where one spouse has died, and the family carries on. Roughly 57 percent of our population over the age of twenty-five is married with children. Add the eight percent who are married without children and you have almost two thirds of our population that would be considered a traditional family. In addition, a sizable number are widowed, with and without children.

Clearly, many dilemmas face the traditional family. It may not be as strong as it once was; it is certainly under attack, even by people who claim to be pro-family. But make no mistake: the traditional family is not dead or anywhere near extinction. However, the urgent need is to fend off its enemies and to wage war on those who seek to redefine and destroy this sacred institution.

Overcoming the Deceivers

Throughout this book we have seen how anti-family agents
have perpetuated the chaos that reigns in many homes. We
have seen the destructive influence of organizations such as
Planned Parenthood, the National Organization of Women,
the National Education Association, the American Civil Liberties Union, and the National Abortion Rights Action
League. These and other liberal organizations are, in turn,
supported by the writers and producers of most television
programming, sitcoms, and soap operas, along with many
people in the movie industry where anti-family films are
churned out daily.

Some of these people want us to believe that family problems are the result of a bad economy. Why? Because they
want to get control of the money and the power to decide
who will benefit. Others argue that such problems are cycles
of change as the culture goes through a process of disintegration and re-integration. This is, in fact, a clear statement of
"socialist" beliefs, based on the Marxist theory of dialectical
materialism, which held that every orthodox view must eventually be overthrown by some newer orthodoxy. Imagine
what liberties they could take, and what chaos they could
unleash, if they could show convincingly that society is in a
constant state of revolution.

To my great disappointment, the most vocal perpetrators
of such discredited theories are members of the United States
Congress, along with a large number of the tenured faculty
members at many of our major secular universities. I am convinced these are the most hostile enemies of the American
family and the greatest threats to our hopes for renewal and
restoration. The record of anti-family legislation in this nation over the past three decades is shocking. Our own elected

officials have done more to undermine the family than any foreign agent could have done. Aided and abetted by the programs designed by liberal educators, such ideologies are already infiltrating our homes through our own sons and daughters. They are broadcast into our living rooms by the media and published in major newspapers, magazines, and journals. Their message is pervasive and destructive, and it is everywhere.

In one article highly critical of the political right, a writer in *The Family Therapy Networker*—a publication that claims to be interested in better families—recently argued that we need to abandon the political ideals and philosophies upon which this nation was founded and expand the welfare state. The article states that the American family is at odds with the American dream. In the article, "The American Family vs. The American Dream," Barbara Ehrenreich claims that it is the duty of liberal family counselors and therapists to help overturn the economic and ethical foundations of the American system and implement new radical ideologies for this new age of change.[1]

Mixed with such outlandish pronouncements is the writer's suggestion that contemporary family problems are the result of a clash between two messages that come to us every day. One is the permissive message that says, "buy now, spend, indulge yourself." This message comes from advertisers, from business, from credit card companies, and from others who have helped to make us into a materialistic consumer culture. The other is what she calls the puritanical message which says that we should "work hard, delay gratification, curb our impulses, and save money."[2]

This puritanical message is preached by schools, churches, parents, and political figures, Ehrenreich suggests. But society is torn between these two extremes, and many feel a "pervasive anxiety, upon which the political right has been very adept at mobilizing and building." The writer claims that we are afraid to attack the consumer culture, so we turn our attention to criticizing social problems such as drug abuse and poverty.

While I strongly disagree with most of Ehrenreich's analysis, I agree that families need to build relationships based on something greater than watching TV and spending money. But we cannot simply strip away one set of negative values and replace them with another more dangerous set. We need a system of values which teaches us how to stimulate and reinforce positive, life-affirming values in our culture; in reality the liberal secular culture has precisely the opposite aims. Freedom of choice for the liberal intellectuals does not mean the right to choose life, for example; it means strict legislation and enforced mind control under a leftist social agenda. That is the real meaning of politically correct thinking.

The Devaluing of Life

Twenty-five years ago one of my mentors, Dr. Francis Schaeffer, made what seemed at that time to be a very bizarre prediction. He foresaw that the gradual secularization of American society would someday undermine even our beliefs in the value of human life. There would be widespread abortion, infanticide, and euthanasia, he suggested, combined with an all-consuming pursuit of self-gratification, wealth, and personal freedom.

Today we can see that Dr. Schaeffer's predictions are coming true faster than even he might have imagined. And his passionate challenge, issued a quarter century ago, is a call that we must heed if we are to prevent the further erosion of the family and the culture. Schaeffer's *Christian Manifesto* sounds a call to arms for all men and women who cherish life.

In earlier chapters, I referred to the August 10, 1992 issue of *Fortune* magazine, with its emphasis on the problems of the American family and American children. One of the writers, Myron Magnet, argued that three forces at work in our society today have done more than any others to change family life.

The first is the emphasis on personal gratification and the rejection of convention and authority, including family authority. Such thinking has "devalued commitments to others made for better, for worse, for richer, for poorer" and replaced them with the radically individualistic ethic that says, "If it feels good, do it."

The second influence is the sexual revolution with its emphasis on promiscuity and the rejection of marital faithfulness and traditional morality.

The third is the radical feminist movement that urged women to break free of the constraints of traditional marriage and family life. These women have declared, in effect, open war on the family.

Within the past few years, all three of these influences have lost some impact as more and more people begin to see through the folly of self-centered gratification, illicit sex, and militant feminism. The fact is, they simply don't work, and countless lives have been shattered as a result. Today there is a violent backlash against the feminist movement which its vocal leaders—from Gloria Steinem and Susan Faludi to Molly Yard—are trying to stanch.

But these liberal movements are still powerful. Even if most Americans disagree with their aims and motives, they nevertheless control the media and the secular universities; they have immense emotional appeal for a great number of people eager for certain benefits that come with "victim" status in the liberal welfare culture. But such programs are unavoidably disastrous and must be resisted with all the strength we can muster.

To challenge the liberal manipulators of public thought and policy, we must be prepared to wage open warfare on at least four fronts. We need a dedicated assault through the government, through community agencies, in our churches, and through individuals and their homes in every city, state, and town in this nation.

Reforming American Government

We cannot expect government to create good families for us, but neither should we expect them to be hostile to the family. We expect government to protect the rights of minorities; why shouldn't we expect them to protect the civil rights of the last disenfranchised minority—the unborn child. We expect government to help those who are genuinely needy, but shouldn't we also expect it to reform and redesign the pernicious welfare system than encourages unwed mothers to have one baby after another to avoid marrying a man with gainful employment?

That is what the current liberal apparatus actually does. It does not encourage responsible effort to improve but rewards failure and sloth. This kind of welfare system promotes the perpetuation of poverty.

There is no equity in the current system. It rewards laziness and illegitimacy but offers no assistance to people who struggle to raise their legitimate children in a two-parent home. I would hope that government one day might provide a tax exemption for dependent children of mothers who want to stay at home to raise their families. Instead of confining children to day care centers, or leaving them on their own as "latchkey kids," mothers could be encouraged to stay home where they could provide the love and discipline America's children need so desperately. Unfortunately, that is not the goal of the reformers.

"If government truly cared about 'family values,' they would ensure that every act of legislation and every political activity somehow worked to benefit the family."

Recently, I was asked on a talk show where we would get the $40 billion that would be needed to support such a program to aid stay-at-home mothers. I said that we must begin by setting realistic and important priorities in government. Government must become more committed to families than to special interest groups and pork-barrel legislation. If we spent less time worrying about spotted owls and snail darters and more time worrying about our neglected and disenfranchised children, we would find the funds and the time to care for families.

If government truly cared about "family values," they would ensure that every act of legislation and every political activity somehow worked to benefit the family. They would lower taxes on families, they would give incentives for education, and they would help to create an environment in which mothers and fathers can stay together and rear their children in peace and harmony. They would promote its interests above all others, and that includes supporting the importance of faith and ethical values and personal responsibility.

Misplaced Priorities

Sadly, we are finding out the hard way—through crime, violence, drugs, suicide, gangs, dangerous cults, and many other addictions among American youth—that the family is worth a great deal more than the impersonal programs and irrelevant issues which occupy most of government's time and money. Nothing is more important than the security of the family, yet everything government touches seems to make life more difficult and increases the onerous burdens upon American families.

Government needs to be reminded that families are the first and most important concern of government. Government exists to make life better for families, not worse. That is its entire purpose. We elect officials to stand up for us, for our communities, our beliefs, our business and financial freedoms, and our common good. We do not elect these men and women so they can immerse themselves in all the irrelevant and irresponsible programs that actually fill the Congressional agenda day after day. They have put technical issues, pork-barrel schemes, administrative details, their own career advancement, and a thousand other things ahead of the one concern that brought them to Congress in the first place. This has to stop.

I will be quick to say that some of the other issues are important and should not be entirely ignored. Environmental, naturalist, and ecological concerns are important; I do not deny that. But remember that nature is also God's creation, and it is wonderfully adaptable. It is also alive and renewable, and it will survive long after you and I are gone. We should show responsible concern for the earth, but never at the expense of our first duty to the men, women, and children who inhabit it. Compared to that, everything else pales into insignificance.

> **"We should show responsible concern for the earth, but never at the expense of our first duty to the men, women, and children who inhabit it."**

Congress should be addressing such things as quality of life and educational opportunity. I am committed to the issue of "school choice," for example, and I am working to convince our congressmen that we need their support in this area. Why should parents be forced to send their children to schools which are inefficient, dangerous, or inconvenient? Why should citizens be taxed to pay for public education if they prefer to send their own children to private or parochial schools? All of my children went to Christian schools, and my grandchildren will attend Christian schools, too. Should I be taxed to pay for an educational institution my children never use? Shouldn't I have the right to choose where my tax dollars are used? Shouldn't you?

Since you pay taxes to support public education, it would be perfectly appropriate for the government to send you a voucher to pick the school you want your children or grandchildren to attend. You don't expect more than your fair share, and no one believes there should be any element of favoritism in such programs. But every family with school-age children has the right to receive either a school voucher or a tax exemption which will allow them to choose the school of their choice without government, state, or local control. That is the essence of "freedom of choice," and the only people who argue against it are those who claim to stand for freedom and choice.

Supporting Our Communities

The next level of concern for government should be the health of the local community. But communities, however, need autonomy and freedom of choice just as people do, not legislative restrictions and government controls. Once this has been achieved, the responsibility for the well-being of our communities rests with the individuals and organization which inhabit it.

Communities need to be environments where families can live in peace and comfort. To this end, our communities must be built upon mutual trust and support. If we do not work together, we are lost.

Our communities need to have positive attitudes toward families. Strong family relationships help to protect kids from serious problems, and intact families offer the best security for kids as they face the problems of growing up. Our communities should provide nurturing environments for families by way of parks, libraries, and clean, safe neighborhoods.

As parents, we must ensure that our schools are learning centers which motivate and encourage our children to achieve their potential. There is no other way: parents must become involved with their children's education. We must be committed to developing and planning activities which continually enrich our children. Together with our communities and schools, we can initiate after-school clubs, youth groups, scout troops, sports teams, and opportunities for participation in music and art. If we allow our children to spend mindless hours in front of the television set, we not only surrender them to the agendas of the media, but we impede their development during their most formative years. Instead we can bless our children by preparing them for the future by teaching them values and skills. But remember, we're competing against the glitz and glamour of Hollywood and Madison Avenue. If we are to successfully teach our children, then we must be creative. Education cannot be relegated to the classroom lecture. Our children must be provided with constructive and stimulating learning activities. By giving our children opportunities to develop their personal skills and talents in "hands-on" environments, a sense of pride and accomplishment will blossom which will bear fruit for the rest of their lives.

The Right and Responsibility of Faith

It is easy to be overwhelmed when we consider the massive problems we are facing today. But mankind has known for centuries that the healthiest communities are those in which there is safety and an attractive environment, and where citizens are mutually supportive, working together to make things better.

However, in our efforts to build healthy families, we will not go very far unless the church plays an important part in our lives and unless we emphasize faith and values. First of all, faith assures us that life has a greater purpose than the temporary and transitory. What I do today has an impact on tomorrow, and absolute and reliable standards exist for right and wrong, good and evil, acceptable and not acceptable. Where else can we learn such values but in the church? And where else can young people and their parents learn such foundational truths?

We need all 400,000 pastors who serve the more than 400,000 congregations across this land to stand up in support of family values. We need elders and deacons and church leaders to make an active commitment to the family and to carry this commitment to the polls and institute profound and immediate changes. We need men, women, and children in the churches and synagogues of this country to raise their voices in a united cry for decency and for leaders who understand their heartfelt concerns.

There must be an urgent call to this nation to come back to God and to biblical principles of truth and personal responsibility. But genuine renewal and growth within our churches must be based on godly wisdom and the indwelling power of the Holy Spirit, who alone can restore wisdom and righteousness. If we are to rise up and take back this nation, we will need the power of God within us. Jesus Christ said, "you shall know the truth, and the truth shall make you free" (John 8:32). When we are empowered by God's truth, nothing can stop us.

When families collectively channel this energy into the local church, we will begin to see radical changes for the better. The support and accountability provided through congregations composed of men, women, and children motivated by love will create the nurturing environment that families desperately need. Parents need the support of other parents who are struggling to maintain their families. The church is a harbor of camaraderie in which parents can be mutually encouraging to each other.

By the same token, children need the fellowship of other children who are being taught godly values. The church stimulates high expectations for young people and offers a wholesome and creative environment for discussing and understanding such contemporary issues as sexuality, alcohol use, rights and responsibilities, and personal values that help people make responsible life choices.

> *"Ethical behavior has nothing to do with taking away freedom of choice or with establishing a state church that favors one religion over another."*

Just as a cord made up of many strands is stronger than a single strand, so families become stronger as they support one another. As I've stressed in the previous chapters of this book, the enemies opposing the family are great in number. In these times, isolation is a deadly thing. So it is imperative that families help one another, and I feel the church is the place where such support groups are to be found.

To make a lasting impact on the way people live their daily lives, however, churches also need the help of schools in teaching moral and ethical values. Historically, the schools have always taught basic elements of right and wrong. So often in recent years, however, people have been made to believe that teaching ethics or common morality is somehow a violation of church and state. Nothing could be farther from the truth. To see how disastrous such a policy can be, just consider what has happened to our schools since the 1960s.

Ethical behavior has nothing to do with taking away freedom of choice or with establishing a state church that favors one religion over another. Remember that the first amendment to the Constitution was not designed to make government hostile to religion, but to keep government out of the affairs of the church and to keep religion neutral. What the courts have actually done in this generation is to replace religious neutrality with the state-sponsored religion of humanistic atheism.

How Things Change!

The entire nation should be shocked and outraged that liberal educators can distribute condoms to our children without parental consent. Children in many places can get an abortion on demand, without parental knowledge, but we cannot give them a Bible or pray with them under *any* circumstances. You can teach all kinds of Eastern religions and New Age mysticism "as literature" without a hint of criticism, but students, *on their own,* cannot read from the Bible or talk about Christian values in school.

Today in many places in my home state of Virginia, public schools are offering a special curriculum for gifted students which, while offering certain accelerated subjects, introduces them to meditation, ESP, metaphysical thinking, Tarot cards, and other New Age philosophies in the disguise of "expanding cognitive skills." From a Christian perspective, this is state sponsorship of religious doctrine, which the law supposedly prohibits. Aren't the types of prejudice involved perfectly clear to everyone?

I realize that things in the past were not always good, but I also know how different it was when I was in school, and the changes of the last forty years have not been for the better. By virtually every standard, the children of today have it worse than we did. Young people are less educated, less able to find employment, less able to compete in a university setting, less qualified to cope with the normal challenges of daily life, less able to succeed in marriage, less able to cooperate with their peers, and more likely to end up as tragic statistics. This is what the separation of church and state has brought us.

When I graduated from high school in 1950, I was not a Christian. I attended a public high school and was involved in everything going on, but we had no teenage pregnancy problem in our school, and we did not have violence. We were not better kids, no smarter than kids today, but we were better taught. Our pastors, parents, and teachers warned us, in unison, against behaviors that could ruin our lives. I didn't go to church and I didn't own a Bible. My father was an agnostic and his father was an atheist. I assure you, I did not know one verse of Scripture and would not have wanted to have religion jammed down my throat. But I learned solid values and I knew right from wrong. My teachers had taught me, "Even if it feels good, don't do it!" And our parents agreed.

A New Family Covenant

In accord with other conservative and Christian organizations addressing these problems today, I am convinced that we can no longer trust that government will take care of *we the people*. What we have learned since my school days is that government has an agenda which is counter to the long-term interests of the people. Congressmen run for office on their promise to represent the values of honesty and decency and stability, then many, perhaps all, are corrupted almost immediately by power, money, bureaucracy, and the persuasive and sometimes threatening special interest lobbies which confront them on the job.

For the least honorable, their constituents become a mere irritant, an inconvenience. The very nature of government, both at the state and national levels, moves them quickly toward an ivory-tower mentality which keeps them isolated from—and sometimes disinterested in—keeping the promises they have made. This is the greatest argument for term limitations I know: to ensure that no one has time to lose touch with reality before we send them home again.

No one wants to impede the good work being done by those reliable and hard-working men and women who are standing up for traditional values. But to keep government available to honest people whose values truly are with America's families and communities, voters must keep their options open and do whatever it takes to stop the alienation and defection of government leaders. If this means term limitations, so be it. We can rest in the confidence that integrity has no copyright. Even if a few good men and women are dismissed prematurely, there will always be plenty of capable candidates for public office.

The weak, half-baked covenants for change offered by liberal politicians will only make matters worse for this nation. Those are not the values or even the issues that matter. We must have a responsible covenant for the family and for renewal, a pledge of moral responsibility according to biblical principles and personal integrity. You and I must commit, before God, to a covenant of change which will bring healing to America and restoration to the American family.

If we want to make a difference in Washington, and in the state legislatures, assemblies, and town halls of this land, each man and woman must register to vote and get personally and actively involved in the battle to save the family. If we want to see evil triumph, all we must do is nothing. If we see evil and do not take an active part in stopping it, we are guilty of the same evil.

But active participation in preserving and protecting the family doesn't stop at the halls of Congress. We can also form citizen action groups to fight indecency, pornography, exploitation, to help the homeless, to fight abortion, and to provide shelter for unmarried mothers who wish to protect the lives of their unborn children.

> *"If you let them, educators will tell you it is none of your business what they teach our children. But that is far from the truth."*

You and your family may want to donate time, money, or goods to help the needy, to defend pro-family causes at city council or school board meetings, to provide pro-family books and literature to your local libraries, or to monitor the selection of textbooks in local schools. If you let them, educators will tell you it is none of your business what they teach our children. But that is far from the truth. It is absolutely—first and last—your business what the next generation is being told. *We the people*, not liberal teachers, must make the final decision on what curricula will be used.

If you see a child in the path of an onrushing car and do nothing to prevent the accident, you share the blame for the child's injury. By the same measure, if you see children—whether they are your own or another's—in danger of moral and social disaster through destructive anti-family teaching, you have a responsibility to react quickly and with resolve.

Whether you have school-age children or not, they are your children because they are the community's children. They are your responsibility because God expects you to love and have compassion on your fellow man. You pay taxes; you are a citizen; you are responsible in the eyes of God, as we all are. You cannot escape your responsibility to the community, and you cannot run from your responsibility to God.

A Mandate for Immediate Change

By moral necessity, we all have a mandate for immediate change. I commit, here and now, to continue and to increase my own involvement in these issues, and I challenge you to do the same. How else can we make a difference?

You may want to participate in a campaign against indecent television programs or to organize boycotts of the advertisers who support them. You may want to start a social-action committee in your church, run for a position on your local school board or political party, and you can certainly vote for pro-family candidates in national, state, and local elections.

Above all, give your support only to those candidates for office who are clearly and vocally committed to the Judeo-Christian values on which this nation was founded. It is shocking how few congressmen have the courage to stand up for decency, traditional values, moral behavior, and religious freedom. Clearly a majority stand on the shifting sands of moral relativism, willing to compromise principles, and leaning to the left or the right depending on the prevailing winds.

We have a moral duty to put those people back in touch with reality and bring them home to find a real job.

We must also get the government out of our classrooms, stop the bullying of liberal unions such as the National Education Association and work for fundamental reforms in the powerbases which perpetuate these agents of anti-family, anti-religious values. We can reduce the cost of education a thousand percent by simply shutting off the federal spigot where these liberal agencies gather. Every dollar we take away from the NEA should go back to your hands, where you can use it as a tax credit or an education voucher to ensure unbiased quality education for America's children without the socialist agenda that has taken this nation to the brink of ruin.

Sam Rutigliano is head football coach at Liberty University. Recently he took five of his football players to a public high school to talk about drugs. One was a freshman—a 300-pound lineman with solid muscle and no neck. He was the last to give his talk and, for a moment, the coach wondered if bringing this player was the right choice. But he was gratified when the young man stood up and said, "You are looking at a success story. I am eighteen years old. I am a virgin and proud of it." If this powerfully built and impressive young man had the courage and conviction to wait until marriage, so could the kids in that auditorium. Parents and teachers must also have the courage to teach these kinds of success stories in our schools.

If we refuse to speak the truth to our children, you can be certain that the other side, with its insidious plans to liberate young people from all moral and ethical restraints, will indoctrinate them with its values, according to its detailed agenda, as we have seen for the past thirty years. Can we afford to stand back and watch? Can we wait any longer? What will it take to alert this nation—total collapse and anarchy?

Taking the Pledge

Bible students know that in the Old Testament, God made a number of covenants with his people. These binding promises were best illustrated by the Ten Commandments and the Mosaic law that God gave for his people to follow. The Bible often refers to the original covenant, the Old Covenant, as God's original promise to be the God of Abraham, Isaac, and Jacob, and of all those who came after them (Heb. 8:7).

In the New Testament we learn of a New Covenant, one that is built on the old but that is better (Heb. 8:8). Because Christ, God's son, came to earth to pay for our sins with his death on the cross, we no longer have to struggle to keep the old law. Instead we can put our faith in Jesus Christ, ask him to save us, to cleanse and forgive us from our sin, and to make us new creations.

God always hears this prayer, He always answers, and He always sends His own Holy Spirit to live in us and guide us when we come humbly and honestly to him. If you have never prayed this prayer, I urge you to do so. Ask Jesus Christ to live in your heart, to show you how you should live, and to renew you for the challenges He has prepared in advance for you to undertake. He loves you so much, and He knew before you were born that you would come to this moment of decision. Please say yes to Him.

This is the core of the Christian message, and the Bible is still the only rational basis for living today, even in these times of rapid change. Anti-Christian and agnostic people will tell you the Bible is old-fashioned and useless. Naturally they prefer to believe that the Bible does not refer to them, since it is contrary to what they believe and practice. But saying the Bible is untrue or that God is dead is no more valid than denying the existence of the IRS. When tax time comes, you still pay your debt.

The Bible is the basis and foundation upon which the American Constitution and the American dream were built, and it is the basis on which American families—New American Families—must be built in the years to come. Ahead of us is a new century, a new millennium, and ultimately an eternity with God. Let's make it count.

> *"Saying the Bible is untrue or that God is dead is no more valid than denying the existence of the IRS. When tax time comes, you still pay your debt."*

The belief system that captured the public imagination in the 1960s has failed. The same liberal ideologies failed in Russia, in Eastern Europe, and around the world. Now we can see more clearly that this false doctrine has lead this country to moral collapse. In just one generation, the American family has been nearly destroyed. But, if this has happened in a single generation, I believe we can also reverse it in one generation—especially if we work together with God's help.

Over the months and years ahead, we need to articulate our goals and then develop detailed action plans. We need to fight for traditional family values, for committed family relationships that cannot be weakened by social influences, for cleaner television and better schools, for the clean up of Congress, and the purging of crime, pornography, and other forms of indecency in our communities.

We need to give practical and personal help to poor families, suffering families, single parent families, and others, without pushing them into inactivity while living on government handouts. We need to teach fathers how to be responsible in leading and providing for their families. We need to help mothers who want to care for their kids themselves. We need to guide kids into responsible habits. We need to care for the growing number of senior citizens. And we need to return to the Judeo-Christian truths that give us moral strength and a reason for living. We must, literally and figuratively, open our arms and embrace one another. Only in unity will we stand against the tide.

The final words of the book of Malachi, the last book of the Old Testament, proclaim that God loves the family and he has a plan for each one of us. But, first, we must look to God as the author and finisher of our faith, the source of honor, and the supplier of the power which enables the changes our new covenant will demand.

I know beyond the shadow of doubt that we can build better and stronger homes. Jesus assured us that "with God all things are possible." And this is the ultimate foundation of the new American family: personal commitment supported by divine authority.

May we all take a pledge of honor to do everything in our power to bring about these changes and, through the promise of divine empowerment, to renew our hearts and our homes.

NOTES

Chapter One: The New Revolution

1. Myron Magnet, "The American Family, 1992," *Fortune* (August 10, 1992), 42.

2. Joe Klein, "Whose Values?" *Newsweek* (June 8, 1992), 19, 20, 22.

3. Lance Morrow, "But Seriously, Folks," *Time* (June 1, 1992), 31.

4. Thomas Sowell, "The New Conformity," *Forbes* (January 20, 1992), 86, 87.

5. A. Skolnick and J. Skolnick, *Family Transition*, 7th ed. (New York: Harper Collins, 1992), 1.

6. S. H. Preston, "PresidentialAddress to the Population Association of America," Quoted in *Family Transition* by A. Skolnick and J. Skolnick (1992), 1.

7. "Single Parent Homes: Children Living with One Parent," Center for the Study of Social Policy, reported in *USA Today* (June 1, 1992).

8. Magnet, "The American Family," 44.

9. Klein, "Whose Values?" 21.

10. Judith Wallerstein and S. Blakeslee, *Second Chances: Men, Women, and Children a Decade After Divorce* (New York: Tickner & Fields, 1989).

11. Magnet, "The American Family," 44.

12. Tamar Lewin, "Father's Vanishing Act Called Common Drama," *The New York Times National* (June 4, 1990).

13. The research on fatherless children has all been summarized and documented by C. Yoest, editor of the study, *Free to Be Family: Helping Mothers and Fathers Meet the Needs of the*

Next Generation of American Children (Washington, D.C:
Family Research Council, 1992), 25–30.

14. Ibid.

15. Ronald Henkoff, "Kids are Killing, Dying, Bleeding," *Fortune*
(August 10, 1992), 62–67.

16. Ibid.

17. "Only One U.S. Family in Four Is Traditional," *The New
York Times*, (January 30, 1991).

18. Gary R. Collins and Timothy E. Clinton, *Baby Boomer Blues*
(Dallas: Word, 1992), 52.

Chapter Three: The Tie That Binds

1   Judy Keen, "FamilyValues: A Familiar Ring," *USA Today*
(August 19, 1992), 5A.

2. The information in the following paragraphs is from Larry
Melville, *Marriage and Family Today* (New York: Random
House, 1988), 4–12.

3. Ibid.

4. Myron Magnet, "The American Family, 1992," *Fortune* (August 10, 1992), 45.

5. Kenneth L. Woodward, et. al. "A Time to Seek," *Newsweek*
(December 17, 1990).

6. Janice Castro, "The Simple Life," *Time* (April 8, 1991), 58–63.

7. Steven L. Nock, "The Family and Hierarchy," *Journal of Marriage and the Family* (November 1988), 957–966.

8. James Dobson and Gary L. Bauer, *Children at Risk* (Dallas:
Word, 1990), 110-113.

9. The research on fatherless children has all been summarized
and documented by C. Yoest, editor of the study, *Free to Be
Family: Helping Mothers and Fathers Meet the Needs of the
Next Generation of American Children* (Washington, D.C.:
Family Research Council, 1992), 19.

10. Dobson and Bauer, *Children at Risk*, 20.

11. Paul C. Glick, "American Families: As They Are and Were," *Sociology and Social Research* (April 1990), 139–145.

12. Ibid.

13. Glick, 139–45, and Larry L. Bumpass, "What's Happening to the Family? Interactions Between Demographic and Institutional Change," *Demography* (November 1990), 483–498.

14. Stephen A. Grunlan, *Marriage and the Family: A Christian Perspective* (Grand Rapids: Zondervan, 1984), 26.

15. Ibid, 27.

16. Edith Schaeffer, *What Is a Family?* (Old Tappan, N.J.: Revell, 1979), 69.

17. W. Kephart and D. Jedlicka, *The Family, Society and the Individual*, 7th ed. (New York: Harper Collins, 1991), 17–23.

18. Ibid.

19. Joe Klein, "Whose Values?" *Newsweek* (June 8, 1992), 19.

20. David Neff, "American Babel," *Christianity Today* (August 17, 1992), 18–19.

21. Excerpts from a speech delivered by Vice President Dan Quayle to the Commonwealth Club in San Francisco, May 20, 1992.

22. Neff, 19.

Chapter Four: Meeting the Enemy Face to Face

1. Barbara Reynolds, "God Save The Court . . . But Not the Nation's Schools?" *USA Today* (July 12, 1992).

2. James Dobson and Gary L. Bauer, *Children at Risk* (Dallas: Word, 1990), 25.

3. George Grant, *Grand Illusions: The Legacy of Planned Parenthood* (Brentwood, TN: Wolgemuth and Hyatt, 1990).

4. Robert Morrison, "Speaking Truth to Power," *Concordia Journal* (July 1992), 303.

5. Sharon A. Sheehan, "Another Kind of Sex Ed," *Newsweek* (July 13, 1992), 10, 11.

6. Mimi Hall, "Lesbian Revelation Rattles NOW," *USA Today* (November 3, 1991).

7. Randall Terry, *Accessory to Murder: The Enemies and Allies and Accomplices to the Death of Our Culture* (Brentwood: Wolgemuth & Hyatt, 1990).

8. Rebecca Hagelin, "Banning Prayer Is Wrong," *USA Today* (June 25, 1992).

9. Myron Magnet, "The American Family, 1992," *Fortune* (August 10, 1992), 45.

10. Allan Bloom, *The Closing of the American Mind* (New York: Simon and Schuster, 1987), 99.

11. Cited by David Myers, *The Pursuit of Happiness* (New York: William Morrow, 1992), 164.

12. Douglas R. Groothuis, *Unmasking the New Age* (Downers Grove, IL: InterVarsity Press, 1986), 40.

13. Thomas Sowell, "The New Conformity," *Forbes* (January 20, 1992), 87.

14. Richard Cohen, "Self-esteem: Sorry, No Extra Credit," *The Washington Post* (June 12, 1991).

15. John E. Chubb and Terry M. Moe, *Politics, Markets and America's Schools* (Washington, D.C.: Brookings Institution, 1990), 9.

16. "Sex Education Is Needed in Schools," *USA Today* (September 10, 1990).

17. Cited by James Dobson, *Focus on the Family Newsletter* (February 13, 1992).

18. Ibid.

19. William Marsiglio and Frank L. Mott, "The Impact of Sex Education on Sexual Activity, Contraceptive Use and Premarital Pregnancy Among American Teenagers," *Family Planning Perspectives*, 18 (July/August 1986), 158.

20. "Get Sex Education Out of Our Schools," *USA Today* (September 10, 1990).

21. Marsiglio and Mott, "The Impact of Sex Education," 158.

22. Joyce Price, "Surprised Sullivan Says 'Whoa' to Teen Sex Survey," *The Washington Times* (July 19, 1991).

23. Quoted in *Jerry Falwell's Action Alert* (July 1992), 3.

24. Carol J. Castaneda, "Suicide Doctor Again Cleared of Murder", *USA Today* (July 22, 1992). Also consider "Defiant 'Dr. Death' Present at Another Suicide," *USA Today*.

25. Groothuis, *Unmasking the New Age*, 30.

26. Ibid.

27. Ellen Snortland in the *Los Angeles Times*, cited by James Dobson, *Focus on the Family Newsletter* (July 1992).

28. Ibid.

29. Ibid.

30. Magnet, "The American Family," 45.

31. William Masters, Virginia Johnson, and Robert Kolodny, *Human Sexuality* (New York: Harper Collins, 1992), 351.

32. "Keeping Gays Vigilant," *USA Today* (July 7, 1992).

33. Ibid.

34. Bruce Frankel, "Pill Becomes Focus of Abortion Rights Battle," *USA Today* (July 2, 1992).

35. Carol Castaneda, "RU-486 Battle Moves Toward Congress," *USA Today* (July 2, 1992).

36. Desda Moss, "Women's Rights Gets a $10 Million Boost," *USA Today* (October 2, 1991).

Chapter Five: Desires That Destroy

1. Major Garrett, "Pornography Is Blamed for Rape, Murder Epidemic," *The Washington Times* (July 24, 1991).

2. The research on fatherless children has all been summarized and documented by C. Yoest, editor of the study, *Free to Be Family: Helping Mothers and Fathers Meet the Needs of the Next Generation of American Children* (Washington, D.C.: Family Research Council, 1992), 99, 100.

3. Ibid.

4. "Abortion in the USA: By the Numbers," *USA Today* (June 30, 1992).

5. Thomas Sowell, "The New Conformity," *Forbes* (January 20, 1992), 87.

6. "Sex Under Seventeen," interview by Dan Rather, CBS: "48 Hours," November 9, 1989.

7. "Facts in Brief: Abortion in the United States" (New York City: The Alan Guttmacher Institute).

8. Tim Stafford, "Inside Crisis Pregnancy Centers," *Christianity Today* (August 17, 1992), 20–24.

9. Yoest, *Free to Be Family*, 84.

10. Janet Daling, "Tubal Infertility in Relation to Prior Induced Abortions," *Fertility and Sterility* (March 1985), 389–394.

11. Philip New and Adele Rose Wickett, "Mental Health and Abortion: Review and Analysis," *Psychiatric Journal of the University of Ottawa*, No. 14, (1989).

12. Yoest, *Free to Be Family*, 84.

13. Robert Morrison, "Speaking Truth to Power," *Concordia Journal* (July 1992), 300.

14. Yoest, *Free to Be Family*, 105.

15. Judith Waldrop, "You'll Know It's the 21st Century When . . ." *American Demographics* (December 1990), 22.

16. Nancy Polikoff, "This Child Does Have Two Mothers," *Georgetown Law Review* (1990), 560.

17. Stanton L. Jones, "Homosexuality According to Science," *Christianity Today* (August 18, 1989), 26–29, emphasis added. See also Joe Dallas, "Born Gay? How Politics Have Skewed the Debate over the Biological Causes of Homosexuality," *Christianity Today* (June 22, 1992), 20–23.

18. Judith Reisman and Edward Eichel, "Male Child Sexuality," in *Kinsey, Sex and Fraud: The Indoctrination of a People*, John H. Court and J. Gordan Muir, eds. (Lafayette, LA: Huntington House Publishers, 1990), 3.

19. James Warren, "The Survey Says . . . University of Chicago Sex Study May Raise a Few Eyebrows," *Chicago Tribune* (August 23, 1992).

20. Maria Goodavage, "Boy Scouts: No Gays Despite Bans at Schools," *USA Today* (February 17, 1991).

21. Christine Gorman, "Invincible AIDS," *Time* (August 3, 1992), 30–34.

22. M. A. Cohen, "Biopsychosocial Approach to the Human Immunodeficiency Virus Epidemic: A Clinicians Primer," *General Hospital Psychiatry*, 12:98–123.

23. Christine Gorman, "Invincible AIDS."

24. U.S. Department of Health and Human Services, Centers for Disease Control, "Premarital Sexual Experience Among Adolescent Women—United States, 1970-1988," *Morbidity and Mortality Weekly Report* (January 4, 1991), 929.

25. U.S. Department of Health and Human Services, Public Health Service, Centers for Disease Control, Center for Prevention Services, *1991 Division of STD/HIV Prevention*, Annual Report, 13.

26. Robert T. Rolfs and Allyn K. Nakashima, "Epidemiology of Primary and Secondary Syphilis in the United States, 1981 Through 1989," Journal of the American Medical Association, 264:1432.

27. Yoest, *Free to Be Family*.

28. U.S. Department of Health and Human Services, Public Health Service, Centers for Disease Control, Center for Prevention Services, *1991 Division of STD/HIV Prevention*, Annual Report, 13.

29. Joe McIlhaney, *1250 Health Care Questions Women Ask* (Grand Rapids: Baker, 1985), 616.

30. Robert Johnson, et al., "A Seroepidemiologic Survey of the Prevalence of Herpes Simplex Virus Type 2 Infection in the United States," *New England Journal of Medicine*, No. 321 (July 6, 1989), 7–12.

31. Marianne Goldstein, "Men Fearing AIDS Turn to Child Hookers," *New York Post* (February 20, 1992).

32. James Dobson, "Focus on the Family Newsletter" (February 13, 1992).

33. Kim Painter, "Lifestyles Remain a Major Barrier to Condom Use," *USA Today* (July 7, 1992).

34. Sowell, "The New Conformity," 87.

35. Clifford Penner and Joyce Penner, *Sex Facts* (Dallas: Word, 1992), 23.

36. Elise Jones and Jacqueline Darroch Forrest, "Contraceptive Failure in the United States: Revised Estimates from the 1982 National Survey of Family Growth," *Family Planning Perspectives 21* (May/June 1989), 105.

37. Nancy E. Dirubbo, "Condom Barrier," *American Journal of Nursing* (October 1987), 1306.

38. Aaron Bernstein, "Whatever Happened to the American Dream?" *Business Week* (August 19, 1991), 80–85.

39. William Wiatrowski, "Family-related Benefits in the Workplace," *Monthly Labor Review* (March 1990), 31.

40. Yoest, *Free to Be Family*, 34.

41. Lance Morrow, "What Is the Point of Working?" *Time* (May 11, 1981), 93.

42. Chuck Colson and Jack Eckerd, *Why America Doesn't Work* (Dallas: Word, 1991)., 4–5.

43. Robert Ringer, *Restoring the American Dream* (New York: Harper and Row, 1987), 54.

44. Neil Postman, *Amusing Ourselves to Death* (New York: Penguin Books, 1984), 105.

45. Louis Richman, "Struggling to Keep Our Kids," *Fortune* (August 10, 1992), 35.

46. Karen S. Peterson, "Grading TV: 'C,' With Need to Change," *USA Today* (1992).

47. Larry Witham, "Experts Differ on TV's Impact on Nation's Morals," *The Washington Times* (June 22, 1992).

48. Yoest, *Free to Be Family*, 68.

49. Neil Postman, *The Disappearance of Childhood*, (New York: Delacourt Press, 1982).

50. Yoest, *Free to Be Family*, 68.

51. David Elkind, *The Hurried Child: Growing Up Too Fast, Too Soon* (Reading: Addison-Wesley Publishing Co., 1988), 87.

52. Yoest, *Free to Be Family*, 66.

53. Richard Zoglin, "Where Fathers and Mothers Know Best," *Time* (June 1, 1992), 33.

54. Richard Zoglin, "Home Is Where the Venom Is," *Time* (April 16, 1990), 85, 86.

55. Morrison, "Speaking Truth," 302.

56. George Barna, *What Americans Believe* (Ventura, CA: Regal, 1991), 204.

Chapter Six: Our Emotional Demise

1. The research on fatherless children has all been summarized and documented by C. Yoest, editor of the study, *Free to Be Family: Helping Mothers and Fathers Meet the Needs of the Next Generation of American Children* (Washington, D.C.: Family Research Council, 1992), 25–30.

2. J. Wallerstein and S. Blakeslee, *Second Chances: Men, Women, and Children; A Decade After Divorce* (New York: Ticknor and Fields, 1989), 55, 63, 267, 299

3. A. Zinn and D. Eitsen, *Diversity in Families* (New York: Harper Collins, 1990), 371.

4. Leslie Lenkowsky, "Facing Facts on One-Parent Families," *Wall Street Journal* (June 26, 1992).

5. F. Furstenberg, "Good Dads—Bad Dads: Two Faces of Fatherhood," in *Family in Transition*, eds. A. Skolnick and J. Skolnick (New York: Harper Collins, 1992), 349, 350.

6. R. Lauer and J. Lauer, "The Long-term Relational Consequences of Problematic Family Backgrounds," *Family Relations*, 40 (1991), 286–290; and J. Peterson and N. Zill,
   "Marital Disruption, Parent-child Relationships, and Behavior Problems in Children," *Journal of Marriage and the Family*, 48 (1986), 295–307.

7. Yoest, *Free to Be Family*, 29.

8. Lenkowsky, "Facing Facts."

9. Gary R. Collins and Timothy E. Clinton, *Baby Boomer Blues*
   (Dallas: Word, 1992), 211.

10. A. Buwick, "Helping Children Deal with Alcoholism and
    Their Families," *Elementary School Guidance and Counseling*,
    23, (1988), 112–117; and Sandra D. Wilson, *Counseling
    Adult Children of Alcoholics* (Dallas: Word, 1989), 63–84.

11. "Assault on the Family," *US News and World Report* (April
    6, 1992).

12. L. Peterson and P. Magrab, "Introduction to the Special Sec-
    tion: Children on Their Own," *Journal of Clinical Child Psy-
    chology* 18 (1989), 36–43; and Susan Caminiti, "Who's
    Minding America's Kids," *Fortune* (August 10, 1992), 50–53.

13. P. Dail, "The Psychological Context of Homeless Mothers
    with Young Children: Program and Policy Implications,"
    Child Welfare League of America, 69 (4), 1990, 291–307.

14. Allan Bloom, The Closing of the American Mind, (New
    York: Simon & Schuster, 1987).

15. Collins and Clinton, *Baby Boomer Blues*, 39.

16. Gary R. Collins, *Christian Counseling: A Comprehensive
    Guide* (Dallas: Word, 1988), 105.

17. Collins and Clinton, *Baby Boomer Blues*, 51.

18. National Institute on Alcohol Abuse and Alcoholism, *Alco-
    hol and Health* (Rockville: U.S. Department of Health and
    Human Services, 1990), 7.

19. Figures cited by T. Mieczkowski, *Drugs, Crime and Social Policy: Research Issues and Concerns* (Boston: Allyn and Bacon, 1992), 2–4.

20. National Institute on Drug Abuse, "Drug Abuse and Drug Abuse Research," *The Third Triennial Report to Congress from the Secretary, Department of Health and Human Services* (Rockville: U.S. Dept. of Health and Human Services, 1991), 15. Also see National Institute on Drug Abuse, "National Household Survey on Drug Abuse" Highlights, 1990, 19–63.

21. Paul Welter, *Counseling and the Search for Meaning* (Dallas: Word, 1987), 25.

22. K. Anderson, *Future Tense: Eight Coming Crises of the Baby-Boom Generation* (Nashville: Thomas Nelson, 1991).

23. Paul Tournier, *Escape from Loneliness* (Philadelphia: Westminster Press, 1962), 31.

24. Mark R. Laaser, *The Secret Sin: Healing the Wounds of Sexual Addiction* (Grand Rapids: Zondervan, 1992).

25. Grant Martin, *Regaining Control* (Wheaton, IL: Victor, 1990).

Chapter Seven: Assessing the Damage

1. Chuck Colson and Jack Eckerd, *Why America Doesn't Work* (Dallas: Word, 1991), 4, 79.

2. National Institute on Alcohol Abuse and Alcoholism, *Alcohol and Health* (Rockville: U.S. Department of Health and Human Services, 1990), ix.

3. National Institute on Drug Abuse, *The Third Triennial Report to Congress from the Secretary, Department of Health and Human Services* (Rockville: U.S. Department of Health and Human Services, 1991), 2, 15.

4. Louis S. Richman, "Struggling to Save Our Children," *Fortune* (August 10, 1992), 34–40.

5. Don Boys, "Get Sex Education Out of Our Schools," *USA Today* (September 10, 1990).

6. Colson and Eckerd, *Why America Doesn't Work*, 67.

7. Leonard Cargan, *Marriages and Families* (New York: Harper Collins, 1991), 82.

8. Colson and Eckerd, *Why America Doesn't Work*, 77.

9. L. Bumpass, "What's Happening to the Family?—Interactions Between Demographic and Institutional Change," *Demography* (November 1990), 483–498.

10. U.S. Department of Commerce, *Studies in Marriage and the Family*, Series P-23, No. 162 (Washington, D.C.: U.S. Govt. Printing Office, 1989), 8.

11. Bumpass, "What's Happening," 486.

12. The references in the paragraphs which follow are from David G. Myers, *The Pursuit of Happiness: Who Is Happy and Why* (New York: William Morrow, 1992), 162–163.

13. Gary R. Collins and Timothy E. Clinton, *Baby Boomer Blues* (Dallas: Word, 1992), 161.

14. George Rekers, *Counseling Families* (Waco: Word, 1988), 104.

15. Armand Nicoli, "Commitment to the Family," *Family Building: Six Qualities of a Strong Family*, ed. G. Rekers (Ventura, CA: Regal, 1985), 53.

16. Collins and Clinton, *Baby Boomer Blues*, 58–59.

17. Paul Tournier, *To Understand Each Other* (Richmond, VA: John Knox Press, 1962), 8–11.

18. Henry Virkler, *Broken Promises* (Dallas: Word, 1992), 1.

19. J. Patterson and P. Kim, *The Day America Told the Truth* (New York: Prentice Hall, 1991).

20. V. Pestrak, D. Martin, and M. Martin, "Extramarital Sex: An Examination of the Literature," *International Journal of Family Therapy*, (1985), 107–115.

21. Virkler, *Broken Promises*, ix.

22. Cited by Grant L. Martin, *Counseling for Family Violence and Abuse* (Waco: Word, 1987), 30.

23. M. Pagelow, *Family Violence* (New York: Praeger, 1984).

24. Federal Bureau of Investigation, *Uniform Crime Reports 1987* (Washington, D.C.).

25. Martin, *Counseling for Family Violence*, 32–36.

26. Bumpass, "What's Happening to the Family?" See also, A. Zinn and D. Eitsen, *Diversity in Families* (New York: Harper Collins, 1990), 485.

27. Collins and Clinton, *Baby Boomer Blues*, 58.

28. Louis S. Richman. "Struggling to Save Our Kids," *Fortune* (August 10, 1992), 34.

29. Walter Byrd and Paul Warren, *Counseling Children* (Dallas: Word, 1989), xi.

30. David Elkind, "Whaaah!! Why Kids Have a Lot to Cry About," *Psychology Today* (May/June, 1992), 38–41, 81–82.

31. Archibald Hart, *Stress and Your Child* (Dallas: Word, 1982), 4.

32. Richman, "Struggling to Save Our Kids," 38.

33. Hart, *Stress*, 7.

34. Ronald Henkoff, "Kids are Killing, Dying, Bleeding," *Fortune* (August 10, 1992), 62–69.

35. According to the National Center on Child Abuse and Neglect, *Family Violence* (Washington D.C.: U.S. Department of Health and Human Services, 1991), 13.

36. S. Steinmetz, "Family Violence: Past, Present and Future," in M. B. Sussman and S. K. Steinmetz, eds. *Handbook of Marriage and the Family* (New York: Plenum, 1987).

37. Henkoff, 62.

Chapter Eight: God's Design

1. Stanley R. Graham, "What Does a Man Want?" *American Psychologist* (July 1992), 840–841.

2. Cited by David Myers, *The Pursuit of Happiness* (New York: William Morrow, 1992), 168.

3. Jim Conway and Sally Conway, *Traits of a Lasting Marriage: What Strong Marriages Have in Common* (Downers Grove: Intervarsity, 1991).

4. Alfred C. Kinsey, Wardell B. Pomeroy, and Clyde E. Martin, *Sexual Behavior in the Human Male* (Philadelphia: W. B. Sanders, 1948), 544.

5. Conway and Conway, *Traits of a Lasting Marriage*.

Chapter Nine: The New American Family

1. Barbara Ehrenreich, "The American Family vs. The American Dream," *The Family Therapy Networker*, (September/October, 1992), 55–60.

2. Ibid.